WESTERN EXPOSURE

Josephine Bain Fauerso

watercolors by Joey Fauerso

First edition November 2012, San Antonio, Texas

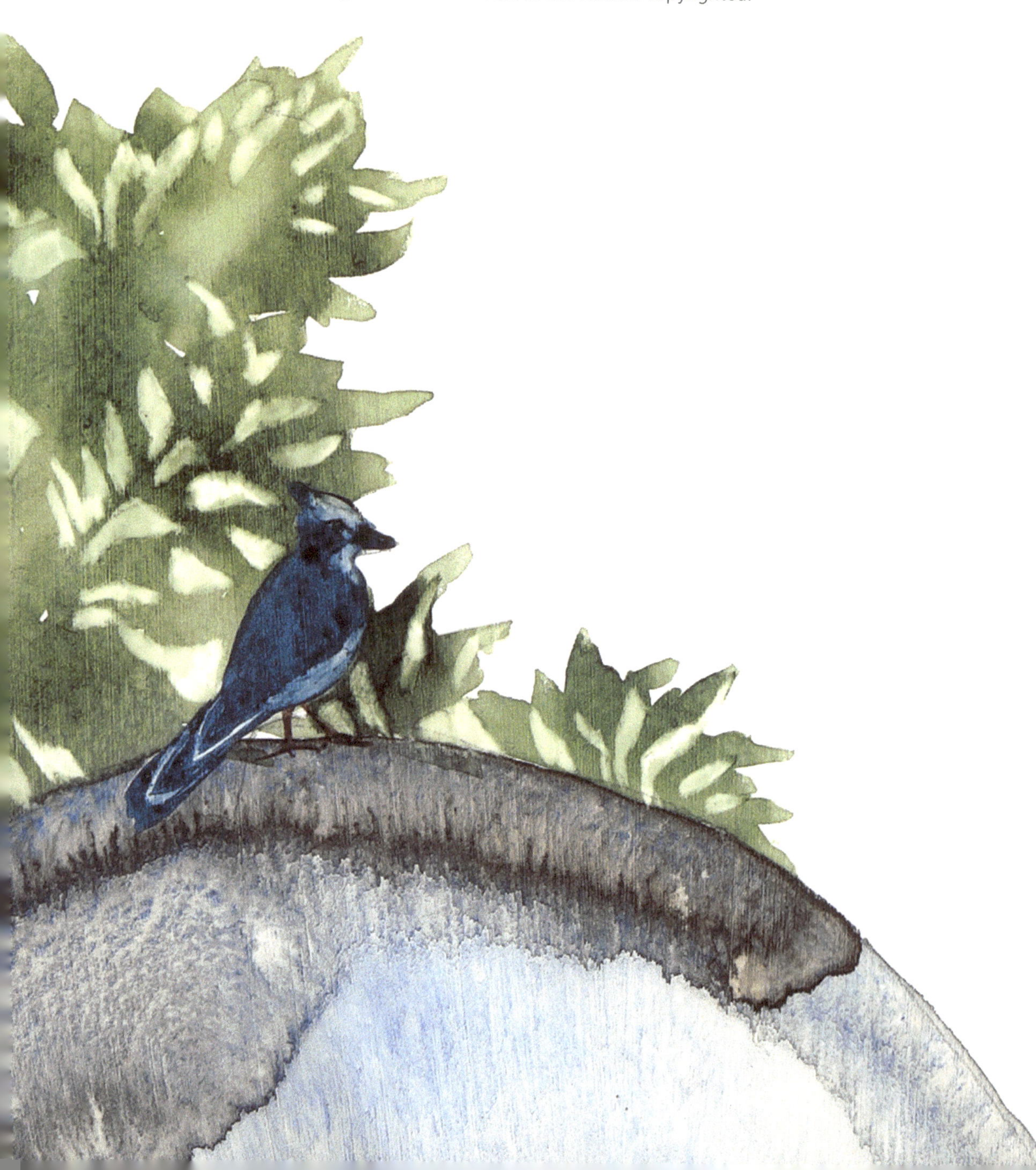

WESTERN EXPOSURE

Josephine Bain Fauerso
watercolors by Joey Fauerso

SAN ANTONIO, TEXAS

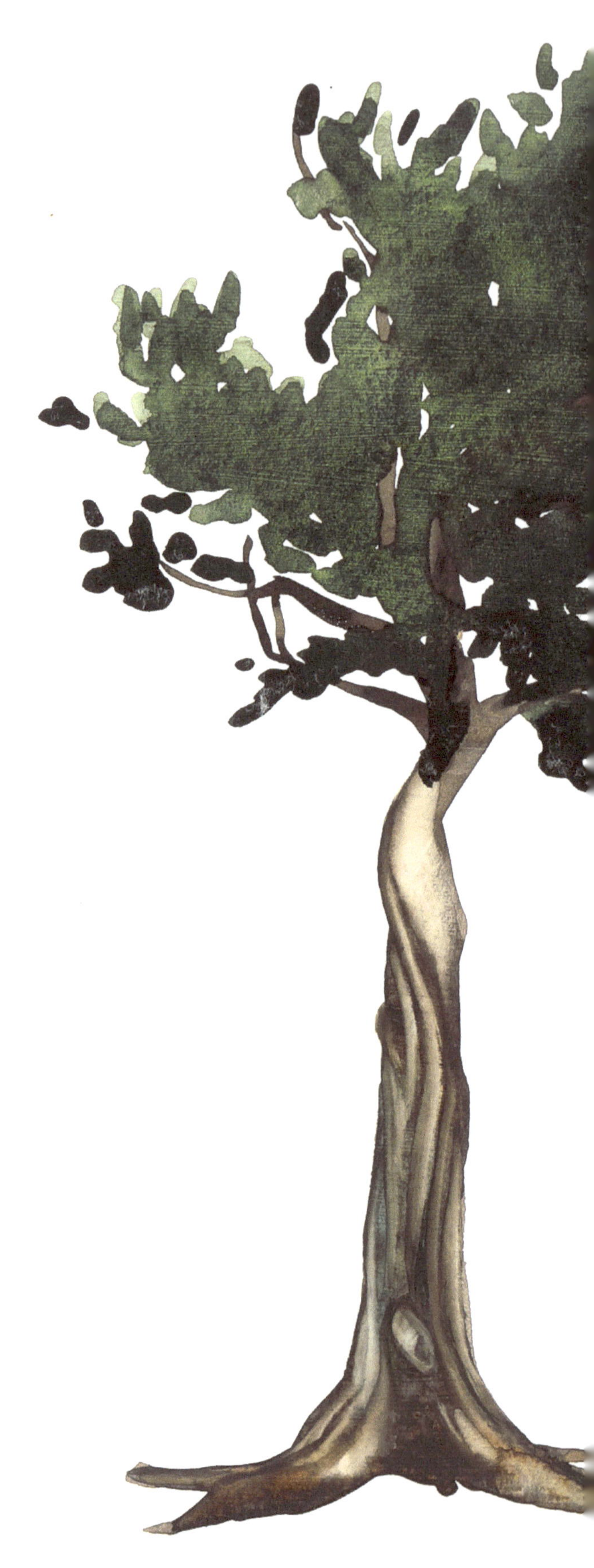

CONTENTS

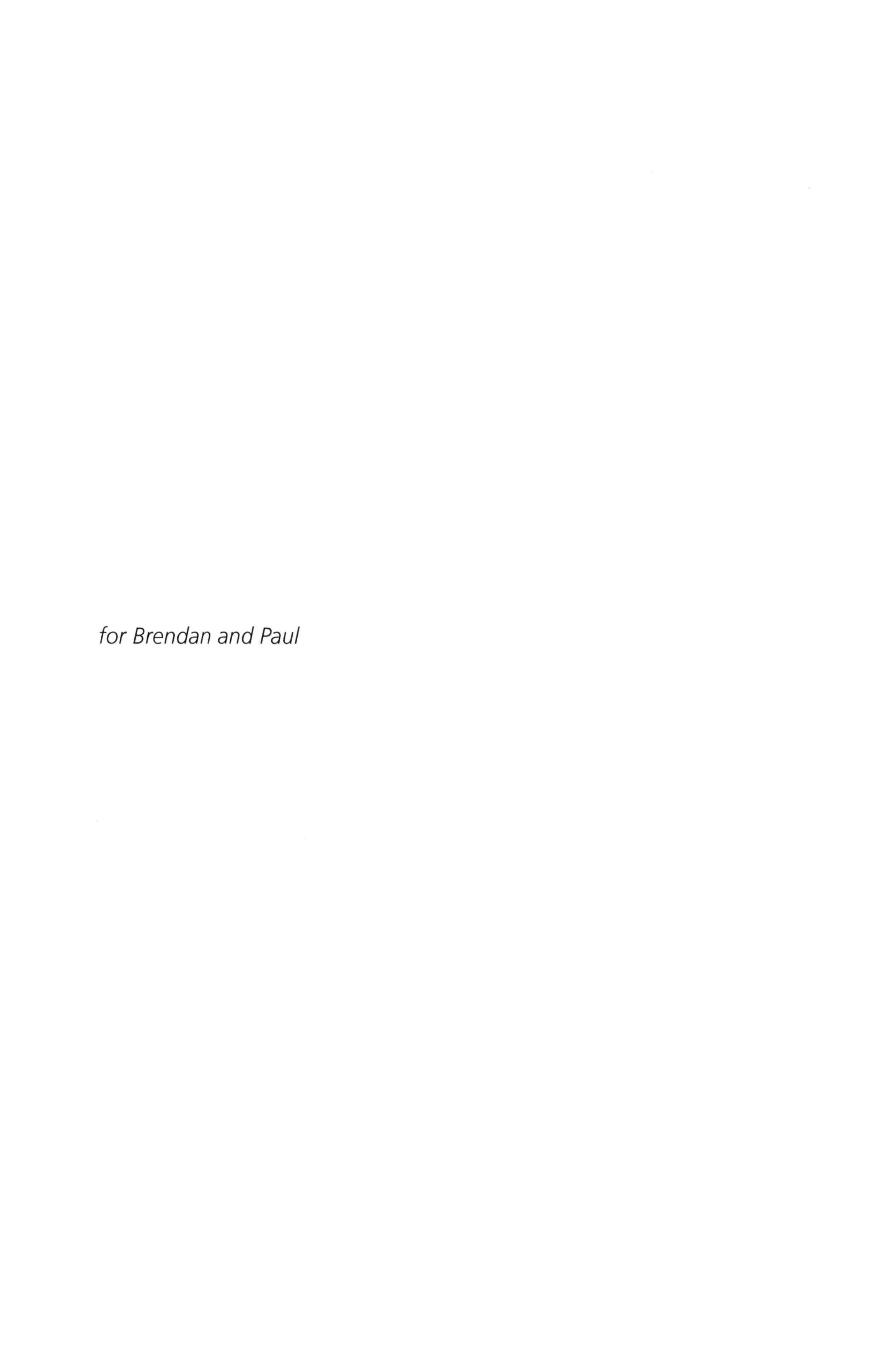

for Brendan and Paul

PREFACE

This book is a compilation of writings made over a period of 18 years. It chronicles travels through the western part of the United States, along with memories of childhood, adolescence, adulthood, and raising a family. The story begins in Texas (the eastern boundary of the great American West), encompasses California and most of the states in between, and ends in Texas with a move back to family lands.

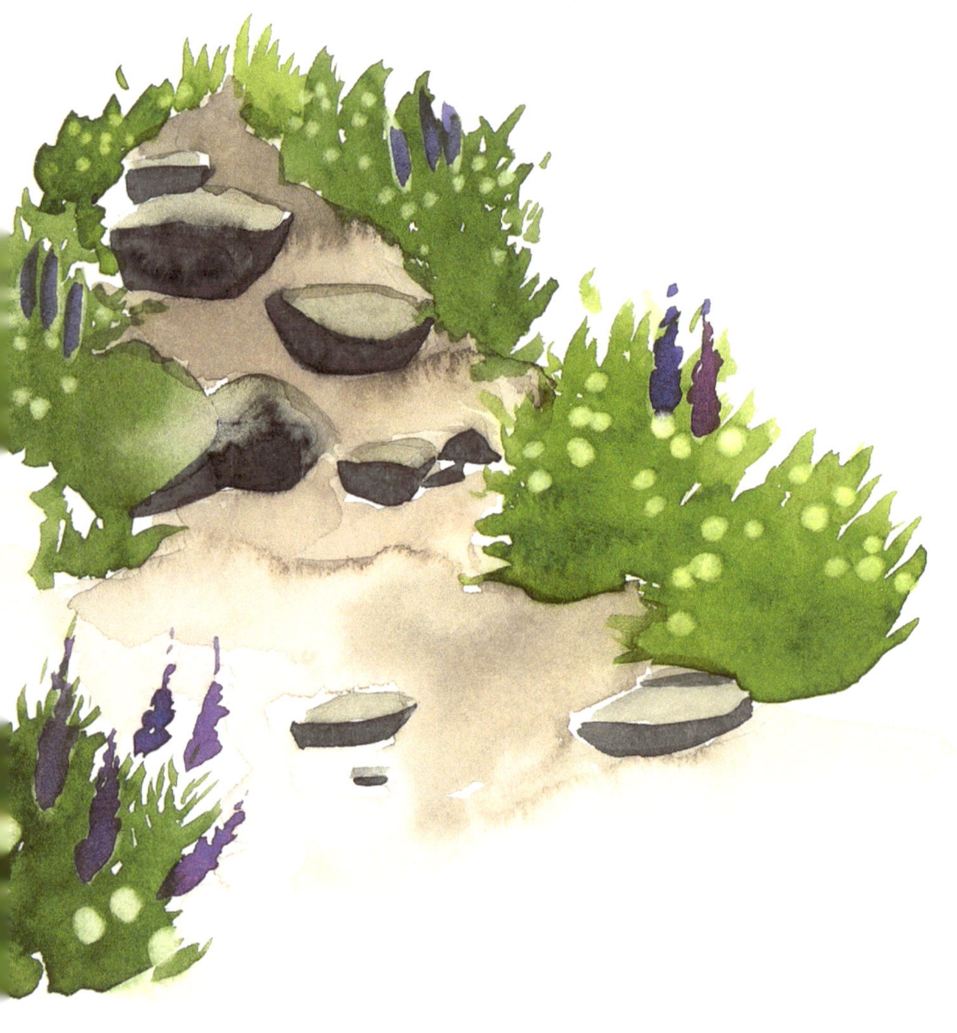

THE ROAD TRIP WEST

Summer 1990

"Save some money for therapy," my friend advised me. "After we drove to Colorado and back on a ski trip, we had to go in for family counseling," she said matter-of-factly. I might have been discouraged as we planned our first major road trip if I hadn't had such wonderful memories of the road trips my own family had been on when I was a child.

We lived in South Texas, which is known for its hot summers. In August it was red hot, and as my parents grew older they preferred confinement in a station wagon with three children to the Texas heat, and every summer from the time I was 12 years old we headed west.

The first trip was our longest. We piled into our pink Mercury station wagon, started out on the old Highway 90 for El Paso, and the road sizzled as we made tracks for New Mexico, Arizona, California, Oregon, Washington, Canada, Montana, Wyoming, and Colorado.

My father loved to drive, and my mother was patient. I learned the art of the bribe as my father, in an attempt to reduce the clatter made by three rambunctious children, offered to pay us for increasing intervals of silence (25¢ for 15 minutes). I remember the bump on the floor in the back seat, which my brothers and I took turns lying on, and the endless telephone poles, which I counted. More than anything I remember the Western landscape with its vast size and dramatic contours.

I remember the fun we had as a family—the jokes that arose out of nowhere and gave us such merriment, and the tricks we tried to play on my mother. My father stopped at every tourist attraction along the road, while my mother sized them up from the car, refusing to go into many establishments. We would return from the burl factories and alligator gardens with trumped-up stories of the glories she had missed. She, of course, was never fooled, but we loved being allowed the audacity to try to trick her and be our father's accomplices.

There was a freedom in being in places where no one knew us. Our social skills were put to the ultimate test: making friends in a gas station with people who had the same kind of car we had; meeting kids from places like New York who had never been to an outdoor cookout (what an amazement to us!); and sitting outside in the summer breeze with our legs curled under us on metal chairs, rocking back and forth as we told our stories to strangers at the Ogo-Pogo Motel in Penticton, Canada.

We went from the arid deserts of the Southwest to the lush redwood forests of the Northwest, from the wild crashing coastlines of the Pacific Ocean to the spectacular mountains of Wyoming. I learned to love the

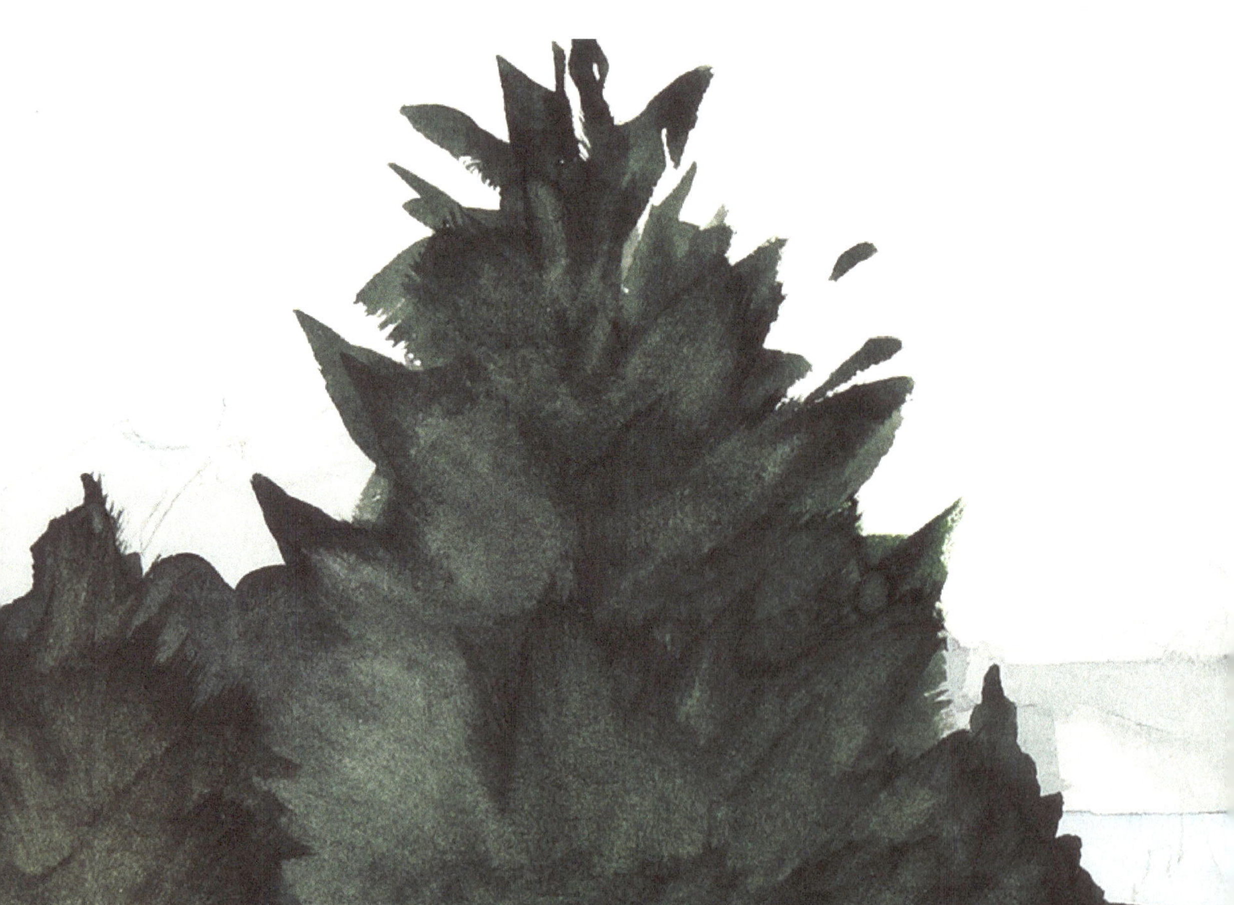

road, the automobile, and the West on these trips. It is no wonder then that I have taken my own children on many road trips, from small excursions up and down the California coasts, to hauling horses around the Midwest to horse shows, to marathon drives from Iowa to Maine and back. Fortunately my husband is a good driver—better than my father was. So good in fact that he will hardly ever relinquish the wheel, and I must admit I don't insist, even though I endure endless teasing brought on by the stigma of a few minor errors in my role as navigator. But my favorite kind of road trip is still to head west—feet on the dash, wind in the hair, kids in the back, we set out.

The first summer my husband Paul and I headed for Wyoming to see the Grand Tetons, the mysterious mountains of my youth, I discovered that he had his own memories to rekindle, having visited them, as well as many of the same places I remembered, with his own family. We were going to stay with friends who have a home in Jackson, Wyoming. We set out from Iowa and quickly passed into Nebraska, a state that pos-

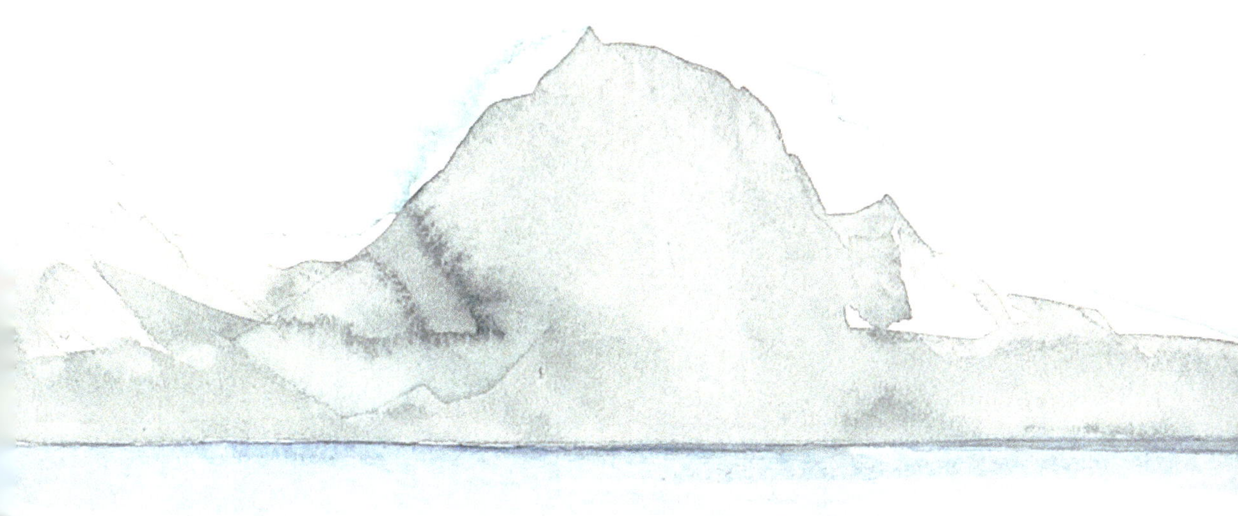

sesses neither the pastoral beauty of the verdant Midwest in summer nor the stark openness of the Western landscape. It wasn't until we reached southern Wyoming that we knew we were headed in the right direction. We entered the Medicine Bow National Forest, which begins with a wide circular plateau and ascends to a very high mountain pass. The forest is completely protected, and no traces of civilization other than the road itself mar the landscape. Tall pine trees are everywhere, and patches of snow still lie side by side with fields of wildflowers. This all ends with a descent into civilization—small scruffy towns in an odd counterpoint to the majesty of the pristine mountains. The grandeur of the landscape is not lost on those who pass through these areas, however. In the restrooms along the way, rather than encountering the usual graffiti, we read sentiments of awe, wonder, and appreciation to God as well as heartfelt greetings from travelers from all over our country. We also were moved, excited, and exhilarated as we entered the Western territories and recalled Thoreau's injunctive:

> *Eastward I go only by force,*
> *but westward I go free....*

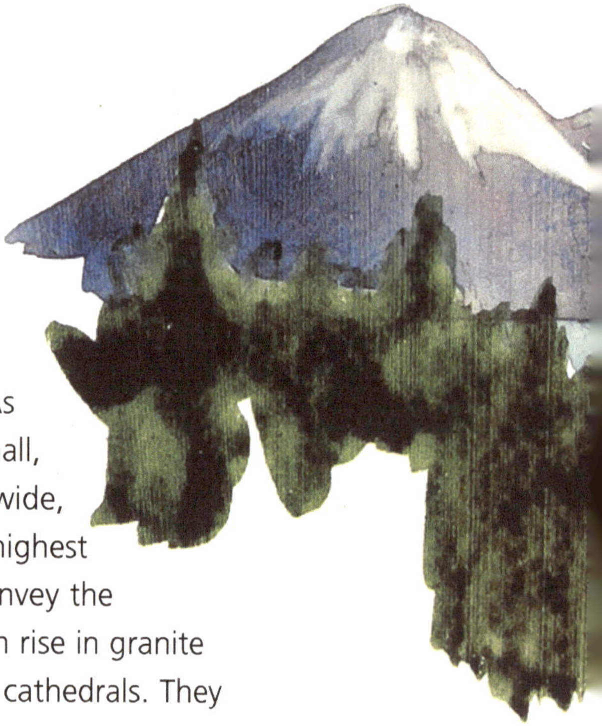

We made our way north, past Interstate 80, which traverses an east–west path from Chicago to the San Francisco Bay area, headed for the beautiful Grand Tetons. As mountains go, the Teton Range is small, about 40 miles long and 15 miles wide, rising to just over 13,000 feet at its highest point. But statistics do nothing to convey the experience of these mountains, which rise in granite spires that make one think of Gothic cathedrals. They are a young range, formed from the movement of the earth and ancient glaciers, with dramatic canyons marking the boundaries between each peak. It is a hiker's paradise—cascading streams, gentle waterfalls, idyllic crystal-clear lakes, meadows full of alpine flowers, and abundant wildlife, all surrounded by the granite peaks of the Tetons.

Our friends were ideal guides to the area, taking us on all of the best day hikes. During these great outings we sighted many moose—truly bizarre animals. Their faces look distorted, with large thick antlers atop their long, lugubrious faces and huge bodies. My husband recalled being chased by a mother moose while fishing with his father in these very mountains 35 years prior. Apparently their looks belie their ferocity, and we were careful to put a good distance between us and the moose families we saw along our hiking trails.

The mountains fall into a beautiful valley, called Jackson Hole, which

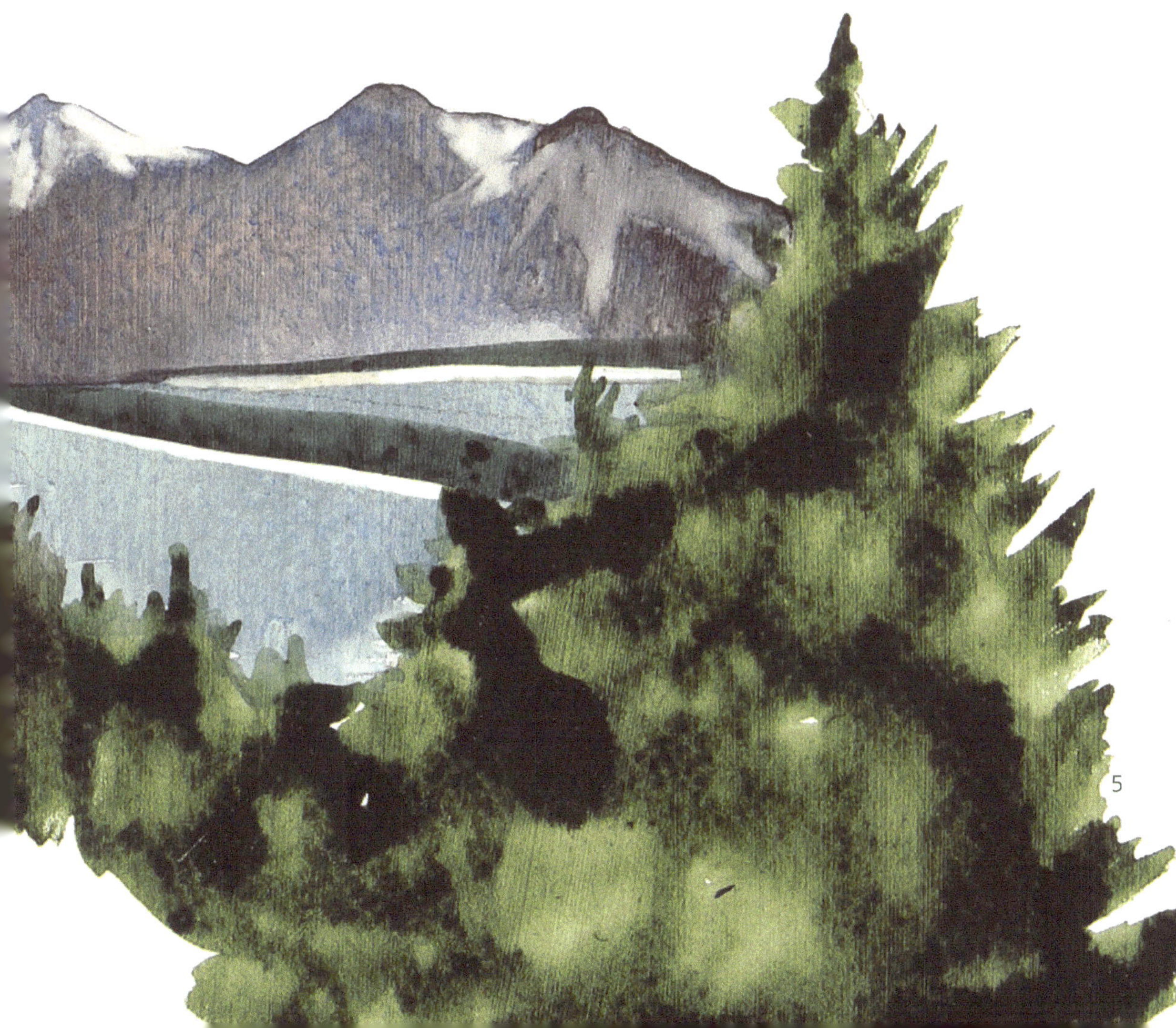

stretches the full length of the range, with the Snake River passing through the grasslands and a series of lakes collecting the snow waters cast off by the mountains. We swam in these cold waters, in Jenny and Leigh lakes. We made a strenuous backpacking trip into the mountains through Cascade Canyon to Lake Solitude—both living up to their names—where we saw families of moose, black bears, little brown marmots, black badgers, picas, chipmunks, herons, falcons, geese, ravens, hawks, and deer. We rafted down the Snake River, wetting ourselves in the wild rapids.

At a certain point in our journey we began to indulge ourselves a bit in restaurant meals and shopping in Western stores for hats and belts we haven't managed to wear since! Then we reluctantly said goodbye to our gracious friends and lovely Jackson Hole and headed north for Yellowstone Park. It was an adjustment to get back in the car. We had been used to our friends' spacious home, the open trail, the river, and the lakes. Now we were once again enclosed in the space of our Ford Explorer, and it took a few hours to settle into its confinement and intimacy.

Our attention was drawn outwards as we came into the Park. Yellowstone is the oldest and one of the largest National Parks, with 2.2 million acres and a variety of natural spectacles to enjoy—geysers, crystalline lakes, thundering waterfalls, panoramic vistas, and of course the animals. We saw herds of moose and bison, groups of black bear and bighorn sheep, and flocks of trumpeter swans. Traffic would stop on the large looped road that circumnavigates the park, and you would know there was something worth seeing. We left our car, field glasses in hand, to gawk at the bears, oblivious to us humans, as they roamed and fed in their natural habitat.

Yellowstone is a beautiful park that was ravaged by a fire in 1988. Fire is considered to be a natural phenomenon, and the 750,000 acres that burned are in varying stages of rejuvenation. Although it mars the momentary beauty of the park, it has not deterred the hundreds of thousands of tourists from visiting each year. My horseback-riding friends tell me the best way to see the park is atop a horse in the remote northeastern mountains, untouched by roads and "tourists."

Our favorite place in Yellowstone was in the northwest corner of the park, at the 45th Parallel, halfway between the equator and the North Pole, where a perfect hot spring (104 degrees) bubbled over into a little waterfall to join an ice-cold mountain stream. It was so invigorating that the rest of our experiences in Yellowstone paled in comparison, and we felt a little jaded hiking around the geysers, cauldrons, waterfalls, and canyons with the other tourists.

We stayed at a beautiful old lodge. Its central dining and meeting facility was made of logs, with a vast interior and two stone fireplaces. Meals were served family style by older people who sign on for the summer and bring with them a freshness and friendliness. We struck up a conversation with an all-American-looking couple whose son played on a professional football team. While we were talking about Yellowstone we were joined by another couple—friendly and personable but dressed all in black leather, with various tattoos and piercings on their bodies. Their conversation was strictly PTA, but their appearance was definitely MTV. They were part of a large convention of 250,000 motorcyclists or bikers, as they are called, who were converging on Sturgis, South Dakota. We were to see many of them on our way home as we passed through South Dakota—on highways, in restaurants, at tourist attractions, and in motels.

Leaving Yellowstone, we headed into Cody, Wyoming, where we found the best cowboy museum in the world, beautifully designed, with a large statue of Buffalo Bill Cody in front. We couldn't resist going in, passing up the firearms exhibit in favor of the Western art exhibit, with its full complement of Frederick Remington's stirring bronze statues, and the *Women of the Wild West* exhibit, which made me think of my girlfriends back in Texas. Lunch was in a Mexican restaurant, in a room full of bikers. The road from Cody to Sturgis was to create a vision many times repeated: the men dressed in black leather with bandanas for headbands and their ladies in vests and tight pants, all atop big black motorcycles that glided like dark swans over the freeway on the way to South Dakota.

Our next stop was to be Mount Rushmore, the monumental sculpture set in the Black Hills near Sturgis. I was prepared to dislike Mount Rushmore, preferring Nature's sculpture to that of Man, but my father's lessons on tourism were still so ingrained in me that I could not pass up such a big tourist attraction so close to our route. We left Highway 90 at Rapid City and headed south, approaching Mount Rushmore from a beautiful little road that took us through Custer State Park—an exceptionally charming area with live oak trees and granite boulders, grasslands, pronghorned antelope, and bighorn sheep. We rounded a curve in the road and from a distance saw the mighty heads at the top of the rugged mountain—Lincoln, Jefferson, Washington, and Teddy Roosevelt looking out to the mountains and hills and majestically projecting their dignity and optimism. It was extremely impressive and moving.

As I learned more about the sculptor who made this his life's project, I came to understand the power that underlies the monument. Gutzon Borglum was an intensely patriotic and talented sculptor. When he was commissioned for this work in 1924, he didn't know that it would dominate his life from that moment on, but he did feel committed to sculpture on a grand scale and believed that great volume and mass have an important emotional effect upon the observer. He felt that this was due to the natural evolution of life. In Borglum's words:

> *I realized that the whole process of life in its healthy form is expansive in character; nature grows from within out; understanding enlarges one's visions, one's happiness, multiplies the forms of pleasure.*

Our understanding was enhanced in a mysterious way by these granite masterpieces, and we shared the experience with our biker companions, who seemed so different on the outside but obviously were not so different on the inside.

The last leg of our journey was the hardest. A road trip is sort of like a Christmas tree: it's a thrill to put it up and a relief to take it down. We were very happy to see the beautiful green rolling hills of western Iowa leading towards our peaceful home in the eastern part of the state. Our trip, however, did not have to be followed up with therapy. In fact the road trip proved to be its own therapy—adventurous yet soothing, stimulating yet relaxing, expansive yet intimate. We recommend it to all families who have at least one good driver, a reliable vehicle, one reasonable navigator, a good sense of humor, and a thirst for adventure.

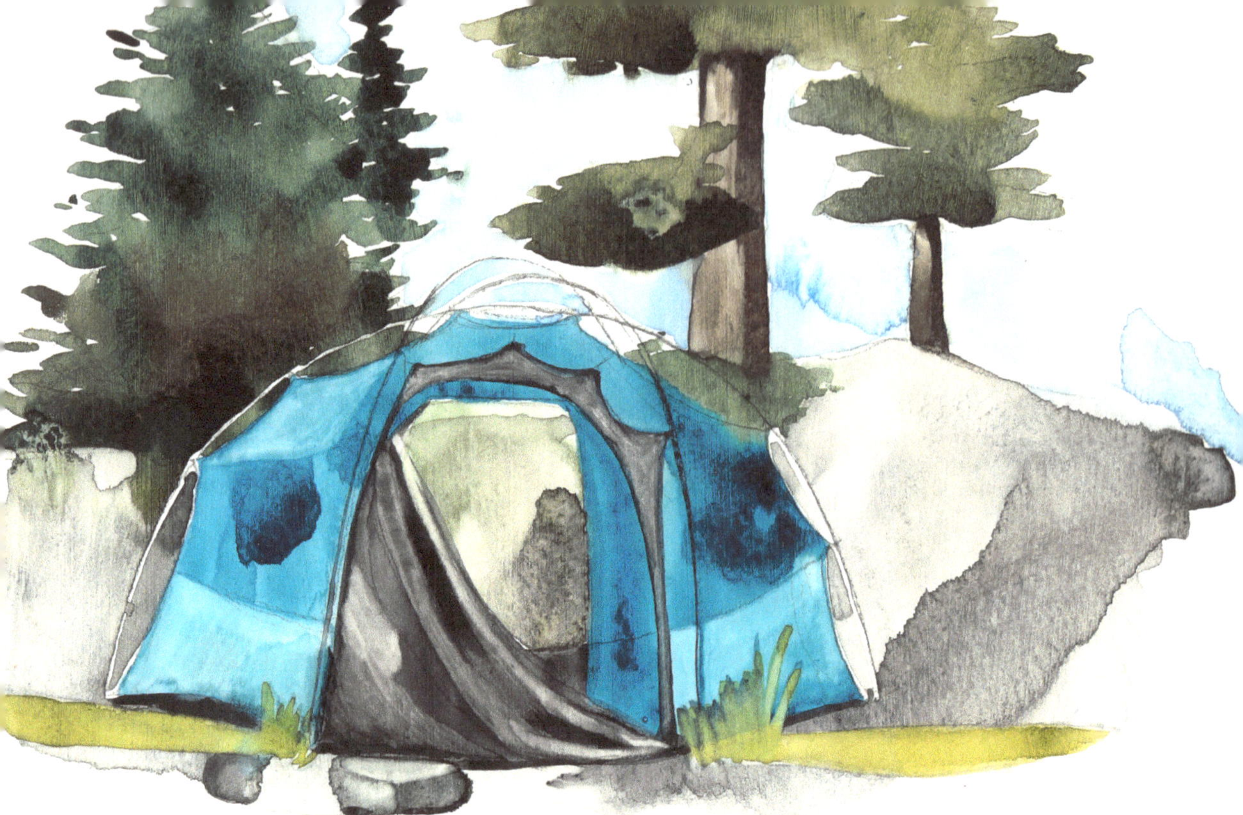

BACKPACKING IN THE SIERRAS *Fall 1992*

Passing through the mountaineering shops of North Lake Tahoe, we found ourselves drawn to the new precision equipment of the backpackers' world. Tents colored turquoise, with aluminum tubing that bends into little geodesic domes; packs with pockets, zippers, straps, and orthopedic support zones; and sleeping bags with synthetic loft which crushes to almost nothing and expands to warm the coldest night in soft silky purples and blues. We were hooked.

For 25 years we had been discussing backpacking. "That's the real way to camp," Paul exclaimed. His parents had spent most of his childhood taking him to the world's most beautiful wilderness areas to camp in an unreal way—that is, in campsites with running water and toilets.

Nevertheless, the smell of the piney woods, the swimming in ice-cold lakes, encounters with moose, and battle with torrential downfalls ensured his love of the mountains and his sense of place there. In contrast, my childhood memories are of the heavy salt air of the Gulf Coast, the jagged landscape of the Texas Hill Country, and the wild endless sky of West Texas. Paul brought me to the Sierras on our honeymoon, and we have been returning ever since. The fall of '92 found us taking a "sabbatical" in the mountain area near Lake Tahoe.

The minutiae of planning and equipment necessary for our first trip amused me. This was an activity that could satisfy both Paul and me—his love of paraphernalia and my love of planning. We dragged our children along, not nearly as well outfitted as we were but seeming to manage all the better. Youth weighs in far more heavily than equipment in backpacking.

Food presented the biggest challenge to us. Those who know us know we love to eat and to feed our friends and family. In this case, because we had to cart the food on our backs, every decision was important—apple or orange, oatmeal or pancakes, rice or couscous, trail mix or Fig Newtons. By the time we were actually ready to start, it was 1:45 in the afternoon, not the best time to begin a 7-mile hike up 1,300 feet of mountain to the Velma Lakes in the Desolation Wilderness. At least we avoided the midday heat.

The first mile was very difficult. Neil, our 10-year-old son, threatened to quit. I snapped at a young day-hiker, bounding down the trail, who nearly knocked me over. But then something wonderful happened as we approached what was to be the longest, most difficult trail we have ever climbed, pack or not—we began to get into the groove of the sport. Each of us went at her or his own rate, resting when needed (about every 100 paces for me!), and enjoying the beautiful spectacle of the High Sierras.

The gray granite cliffs and rocks formed a backdrop to the cobalt blue sky and towering pine and spruce trees. Desolation Wilderness alternates between barren granite cliffs and intense forest beauty. Our trail wound along, climbing one ridge after another, sometimes traversing the clear open side of the mountain and other times disappearing into the forest. We climbed boulders, crossed streams, navigated narrow paths carved into precipices. We learned to rest on rocks that slanted slightly upwards to support our packs as we sat. Sometimes we would just rest the pack while still standing. We drank water frequently and ate our PowerBars, which are full of the right kind of carbohydrate energy. We tried to breathe through our noses instead of huffing and puffing, but there were times when the H and P's couldn't be avoided.

Joey, our 16-year-old daughter, bounded ahead with her long strong legs carrying her to the top of the first mountain before any of the rest of us. She took her pack off and doubled back. "Mom, you'll never make it." Whether that was true or not, I was grateful for relief, and I gave her my pack and took Neil's. We made it up without trouble. Two girls walking down were shaking their heads. "You're not anywhere near the Velma Lakes. We left 2 hours ago and we've been coming down." Nevertheless we pressed on. After Joey picked up her pack and I resumed mine, we came to a less strenuous, more barren area. My family left me in the rear and slowly hiked away from me, out of my vision and earshot.

I was alone in the Desolation Wilderness, 4 miles up and away from the trailhead. The silence and wind and granite rocks surrounded me. What if my ankles gave out and I fell? How would they know? Probably at sunset they would realize I had perished on the trail and come back to make arrangements to have me carted down the mountain. But wait! Wasn't I the woman who had just climbed this mountain with a 30-pound pack? Why should I be afraid of this lonely landscape? This was what I had come after.

Just as my fears were being overcome, I started down an incline that was considerably more forested and friendly, and a beautiful blue lake peeked at me from below. I still couldn't see my family but trusted that they were guided by the same vision as mine. As I finally made my way to the little lake, I could hear them calling me in the distance. I was so tired I didn't know if I could make it, but I really had no choice but to continue. When I got to their location, I sat down, took my backpack and boots off, and immersed my feet in the cold, cold water. I would go no further, not one step.

Next to the lake, my family had found the ideal campsite, encircled by a granite rock that provided a kitchen and a level area for the tent. We began to set up our camp. Dinner that night was cooked in the dark—this is what happens to late backpackers. No fires were permitted in these wilderness areas, due to a drought that had continued for 7 years. Food, cooking equipment, and supplies had to be suspended from tree branches 25 feet above the ground to discourage bears from raiding the campsites. Paul and Neil accomplished this feat in the dark, propelled by our intense desire not to encounter these animals near our tent.

That Sierra night gave us a panorama I'd never seen before—stars so close, so dense, and so brilliant they pierced our hearts with wonder and awe. As tired as I was, I kept poking my head outside the tent to take in the celestial quietude and beauty—one of the rewards of the backpacker.

We slept four in a row on little air mattresses, snuggled in our high-loft sleeping bags. I would awake every hour or so—not used to these sleeping conditions—and enjoy the quiet, encapsulated feeling of our dome tent and the sweet cold fresh air.

The next morning we "bathed" in the lake with a morning swim and spent 2 hours, novice campers that we were, making the most delicious pancakes we had ever eaten. The descent proved only slightly easier than the ascent, but our wearied knees and ankles were soothed by a last-minute swim in Eagle Lake on the way down.

Back home my friends were impressed but unmoved when I recounted the joys of backpacking. "Josie, I like to hike, but that's as far as it goes. I must have a warm bed and clean sheets at the end of the day." Others were incredulous that this would be enjoyable for anyone. But I found others who themselves have packed around the world, from circumvent-

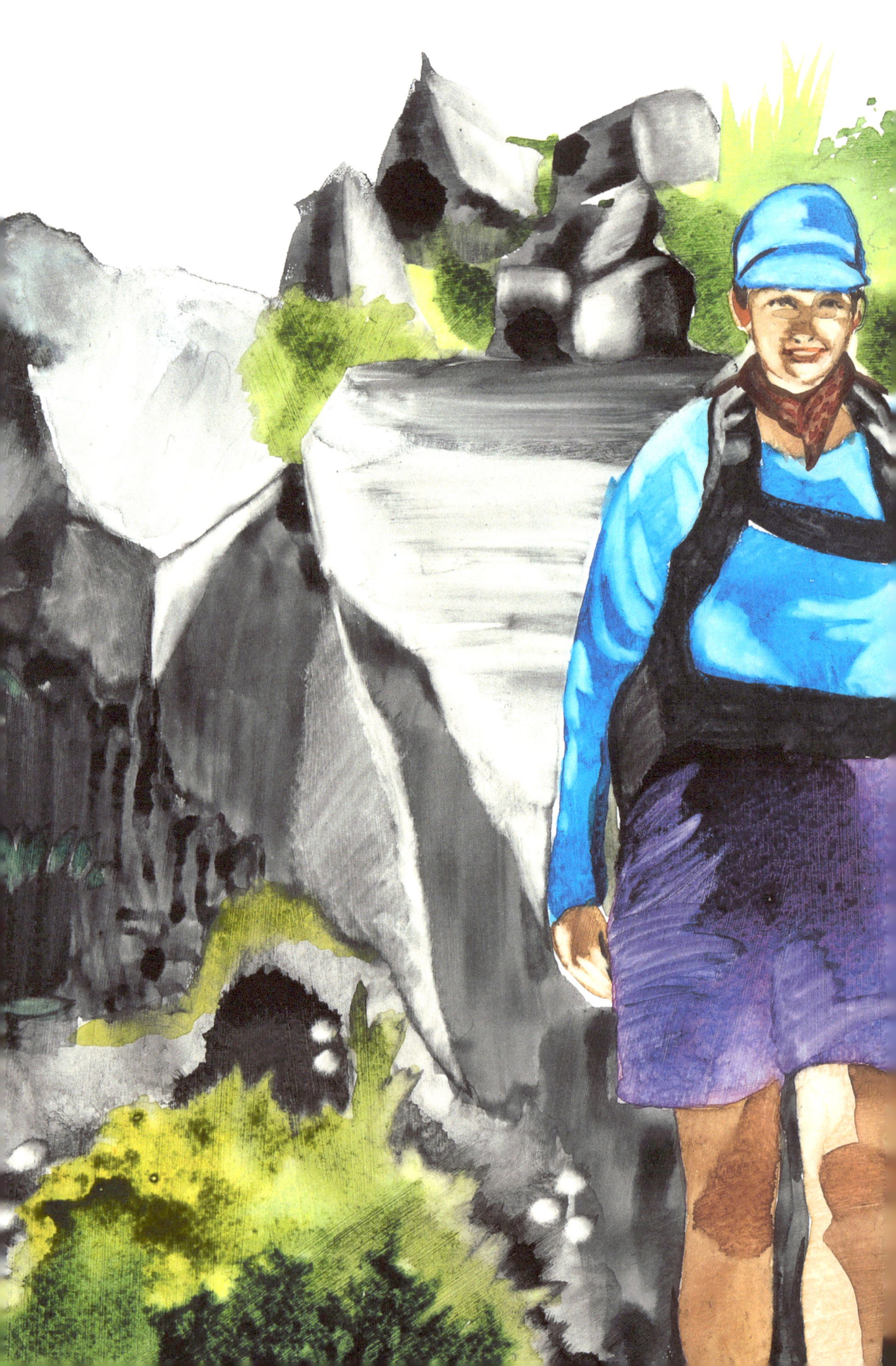

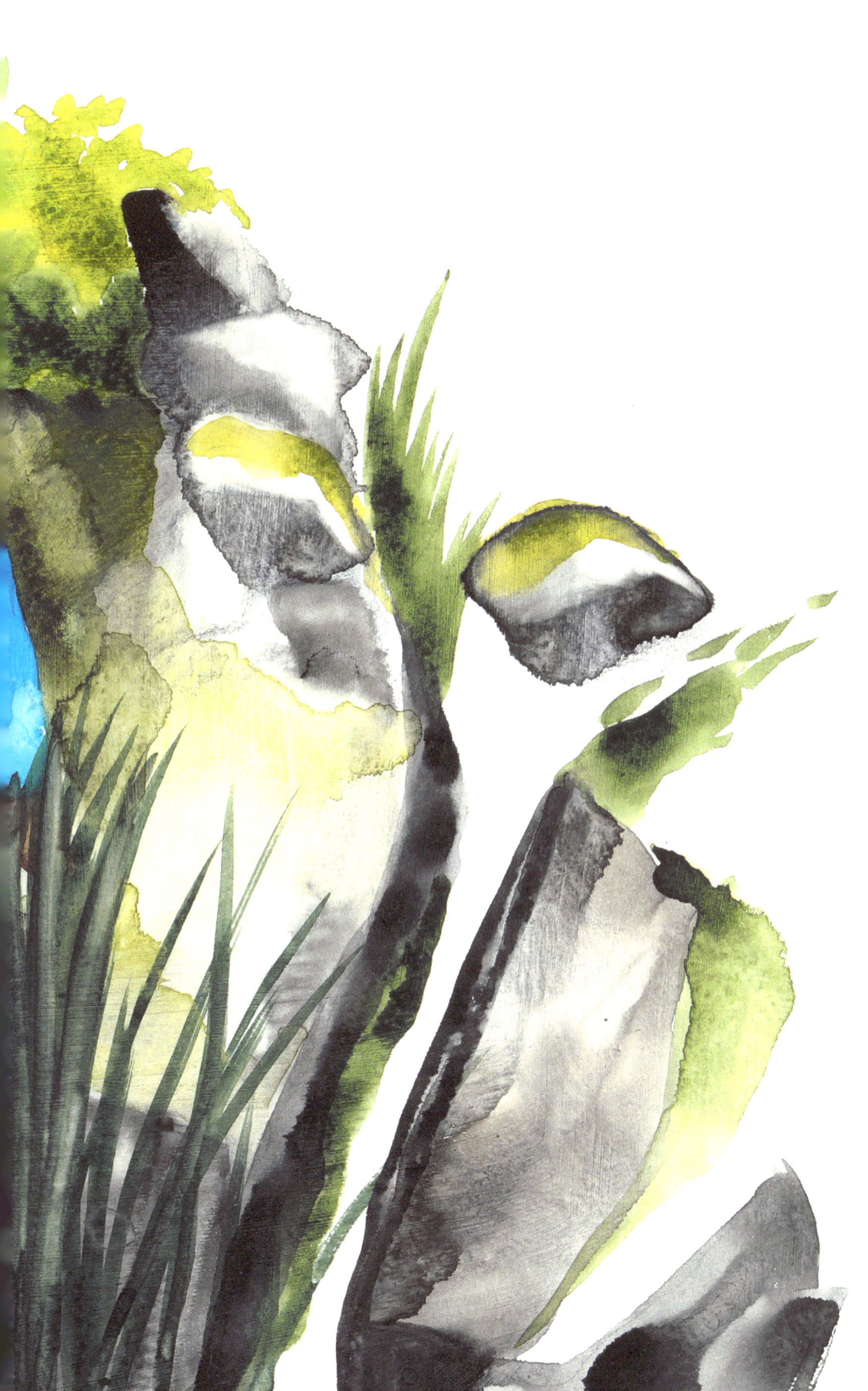

ing Mont Blanc to getting lost in the Missouri Wilderness.

I can only say that for a person in her forties, backpacking is much cheaper than a sports car, far less dangerous than a motorcycle, and still gives the thrill of accomplishing something unexpected and stimulating.

We made a second trip to the Upper Loch Leven Lake a few weeks later, with similar success. I also accompanied Neil to Yosemite for 5 days of camping with 54 children; that was difficult and a story for another day.

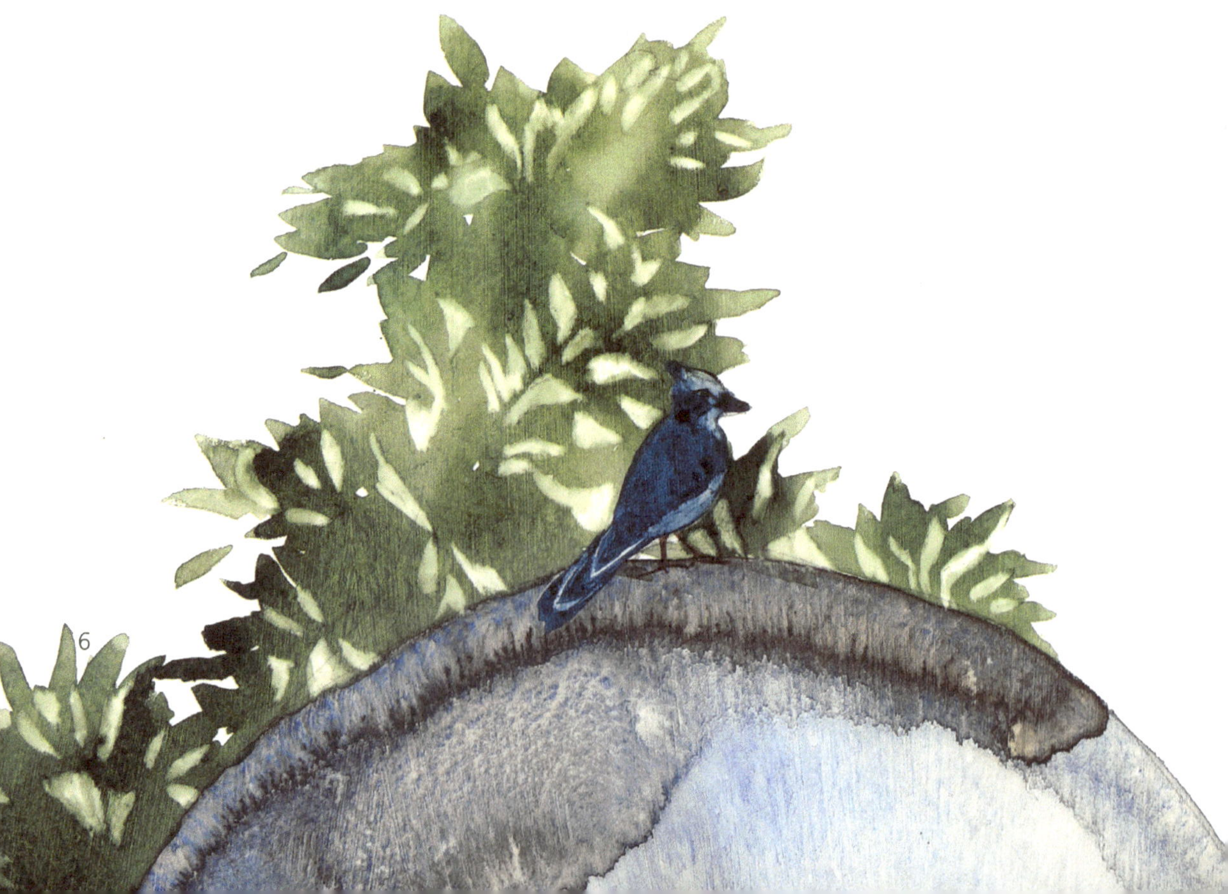

YOSEMITE REVISITED

Fall 1993

Just over a year ago I left our warm cabin in Lake Tahoe for an adventure I'll never forget. I would accompany my 10-year-old son's class and another companion class on a 5-day camping trip to Yosemite National Park in Northern California. The chance to see Yosemite in the fall was irresistible: to camp beneath the granite cliffs of El Capitan and Half Dome, to bathe in the ice-cold rivers that meander through the valleys, to climb the cliffs next to the cascading waterfalls, to see the forests shedding their autumn colors. I would introduce Neil to the region, which has inspired awe in John Muir, Teddy Roosevelt, and the 3 million people who visit it every year. The trip turned out to be all I expected and much more, too much more—a 7 AM-to-11 PM marathon that included the full range of human experience possible in a campsite with 54 boisterous and energetic children.

We began in a caravan. The food for the troops, all planned in minute detail, was crammed into the many vehicles driven by parents and teachers. It was a 5-hour trip past Mono Lake, and it climbed 7,000 feet to a high mountain pass. We entered the park through the north, passing through Tuolumne Meadows—an alpine meadow—which is home to wildflowers, rivers, and trailheads for hikes leading to the high granite mountains that border it. Wonder after wonder enveloped us as we made our way through the 1,189-square-mile park. The granite in Yosemite seems alive, conveying massive strength and timeless continuity.

Its shapes and contours form cliffs and mountains that frame the 6-mile-long valley at the center of the park, where we were headed.

The drama of the mountain drive gave way to meadows lined with aspens and pines as we descended into the valley and found the group campsite at North Pines. The task of unloading food for 70 for 5 days, plus the 20 tents, sleeping bags, clothes, and stoves, would have been demanding on its own. We were staying in a "walk in" camp, which means no cars are allowed near the campsites. The task changed from demanding to strenuous as we hauled our gear across the river (far easier than following the winding trail) by hopping onto stones and climbing up riverbanks. After driving 5 hours and unloading boxes, crates, and bags, I had to set up my tent—a task I hadn't done before. I was highly motivated, for it afforded the only measure of privacy in sight. I should have been tipped off by the composed-looking mothers who announced they were staying in the tent cabins next to the showers, the only showers to be had, 15 minutes from our campsite.

Dinner that night was a Herculean task that included storing all of the food in locked steel bins to deter the 350 resident bears from raiding the campsite. It was pitch dark before the children were finally fed. They brushed their teeth and stored even their toothpaste in the steel bins. Sleeping was not a problem that night. In fact, it was to become my favorite part of the day, giving me the rest that was utterly missing from my many active hours of preparing meals for the children, leading hikes, listening to instructions from the teachers, checking up on the kids in my group, monitoring bathroom and bedtime activities, and checking the tents for items the bears might be interested in. Who would have thought the wilderness could be so hectic?

The days began at 7 AM, with breakfast. The mothers then made lunch sandwiches and cleaned up breakfast while we got our daily schedule. That first day it involved visits to the Indian Village and Museum, Ansel Adams Gallery, and the Awanhee Hotel. After shepherding five children to these places, I required a break. We swam in the river—it was so cold it took our breath away—and only the heartiest children really immersed themselves: spunky little raven-haired Sylvia from Chile; intrepid T.W., who was a strong blond California boy; and of course Neil and me—Midwestern fools. It was refreshing, my bath of the day, but it made us late for the afternoon walk with the Ranger and initiated a pattern of lateness I couldn't avoid for the rest of the trip. How I wished for the freedom to say "Let's have a game of cards in our tents!"

Dinners required energetic labor from the mothers—the fathers mysteriously disappeared at this time, only to reappear at nightfall when most of the work was completed—led by the tireless teacher who barely slept. As she said, "sleep is not my thing." None of us could keep up with her, though she was in her sixties and afflicted with a limp. It turned out that quietness was what I missed most—not showers, not food, not the telephone, not my bed, just quietness—the restful rhythms of my life that are like a backdrop to all the surface action. There in Yosemite, it was all action!

The second day found us mounting the difficult trail to Vernal Falls. My group divided, half speeding ahead, led by T.W., and half lagging behind, entertained by Sylvia's jokes. I didn't know what to do; I could not force either end to more moderation. I stayed with the slow ones until another faster group on the descent passed us. When they agreed to accompany the dawdlers back to camp, I could speed ahead to join my lively boys.

The mountain was so beautiful it was heart stopping, with a waterfall and raging river at the center of a steel-gray granite cliff. We climbed steep stone stairs to the top of the falls. The drought had cut the flow of water greatly, exposing rounded granite banks that formed the pools above the falls. "Water slides!" screamed the boys as they bolted. It took all of my effort to collect them and keep them from slipping into the deep pools above the dangerous falls. My feelings were mixed—love of

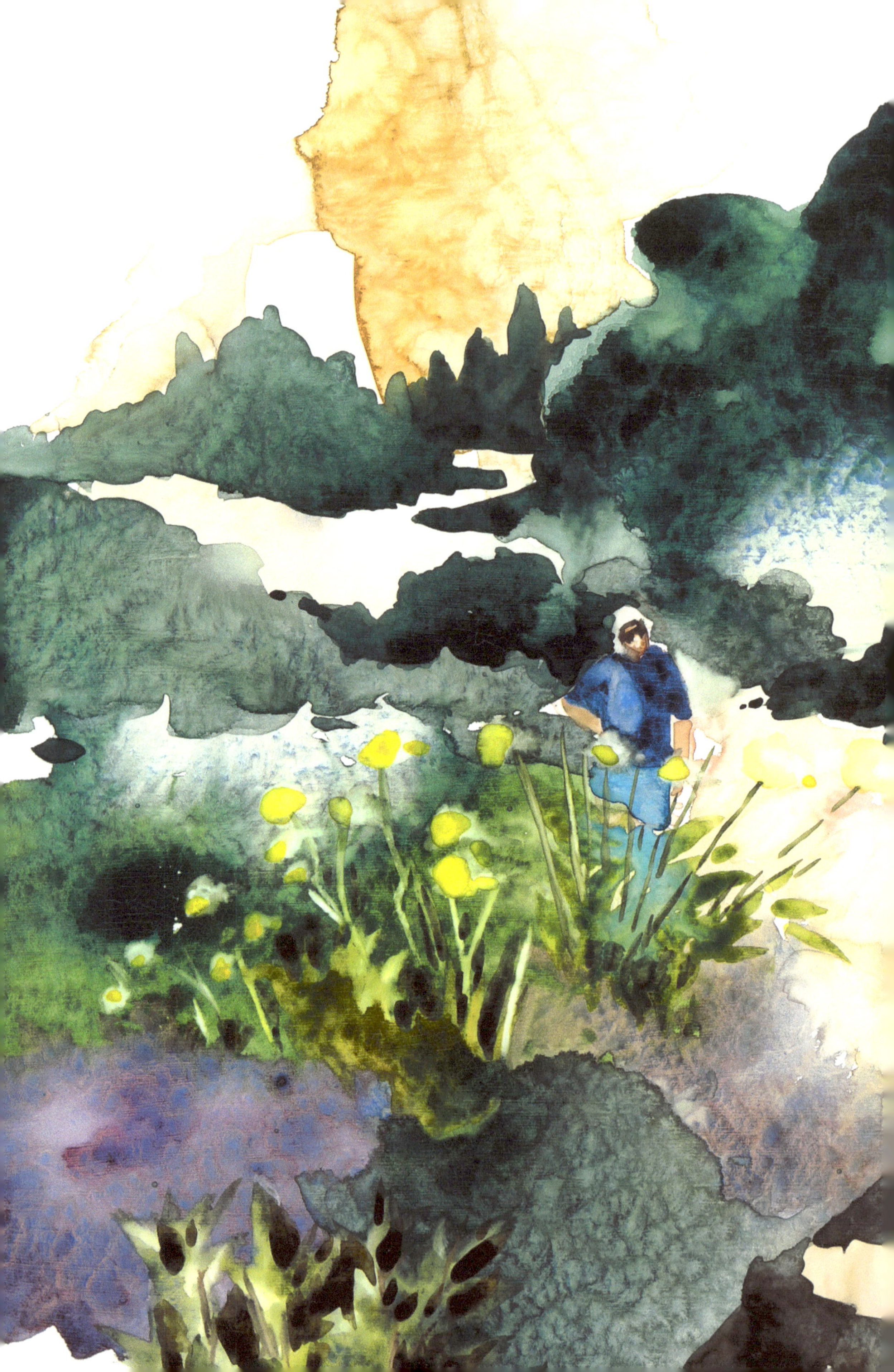

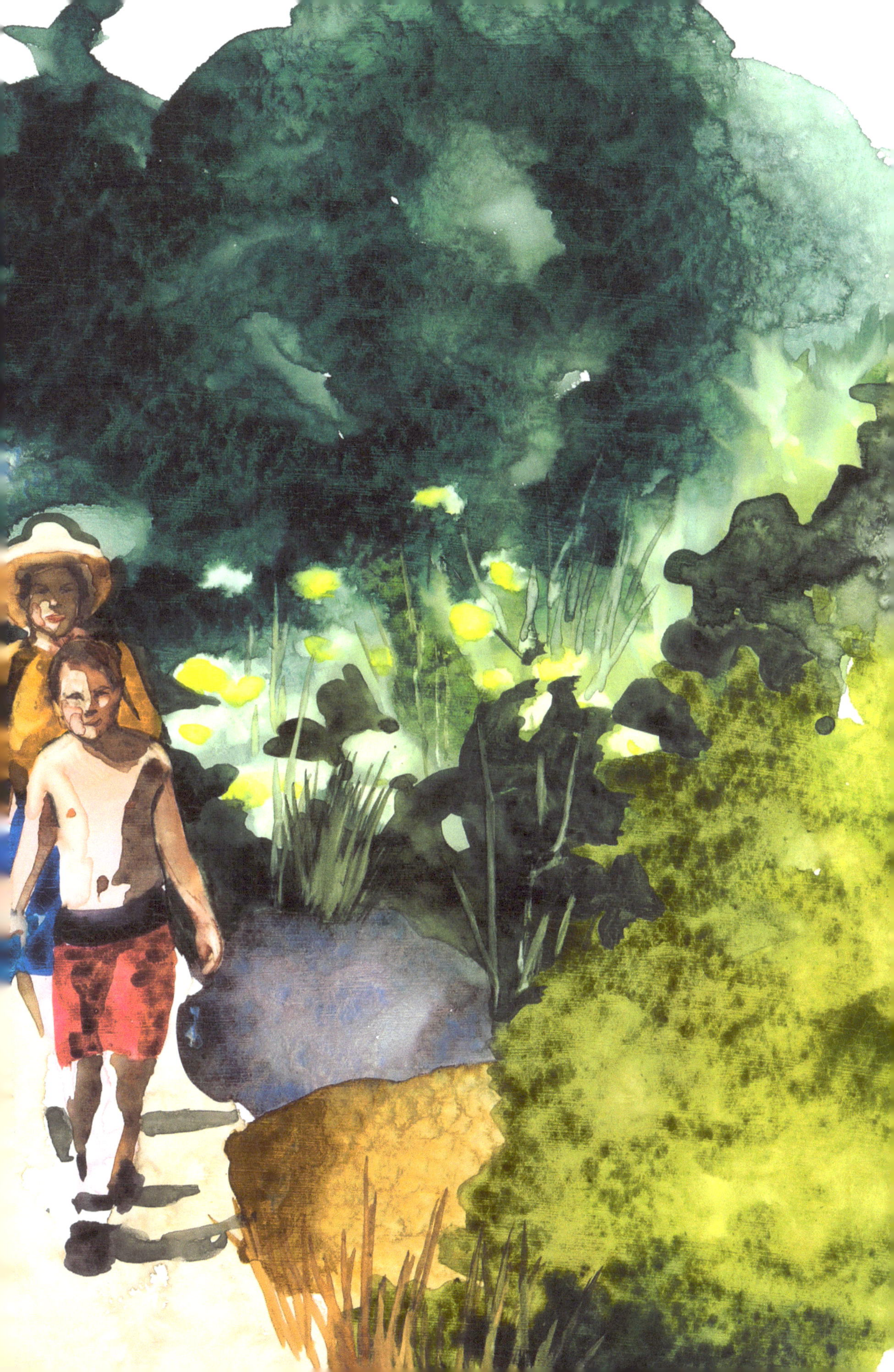

the mountains and adventure along with apprehension for the safety of the children in my charge. I thought of the other parents, at the swimming pool by now with the rest of the children. Yet the thrilling natural beauty at hand was like a magnet, and by the time I could pull the boys and myself away I was once again LATE.

Dinners became more civilized as we started to form a routine. The children were fed while it was still light (a big advantage). They were in their tents as the Sierra night unveiled its splendors. I made the rounds of all the tents to check for food the boys secretly left out to attract the bears. The teacher's warnings had not made an impression on the children, and they must have slept too soundly to hear the middle-of-the-night screams I ascribed to the bears. I understood, as the boys did not, how dangerous it would be to have those animals in our camp.

Many parents accompanied us on the trip, but by far the most interesting was the Australian rancher and pilot, Frazier. He had the frank, open quality many Australians have and was full of stories of the outback and facts of great interest to 5th-grade boys—snake populations of the Amazon, hunting and trekking habits of the Aborigines, etc. He was an Australian expatriate, citing the "socialist" government and overtaxing of his properties as his reasons for leaving his country. He had grown up on a big ranch in the Outback and wielded a whip as well as Crocodile Dundee himself. At dusk he demonstrated his skills, his whip raising dust on the children as they circled round him. I would talk to him and some of the other parents after the camp was settled and the children were in their tents. Conversation was lively because Frazier had an opinion about everything. I always stayed up too late, but I spent my evenings joking and talking with this group of parents because I felt lonesome. All that relentless work without the luxury of phones or showers required the antidote of pleasant company those evenings provided.

One evening I took the children to a program called Yosemite Live. It was a play about the naturalist John Muir, who loved the Yosemite

Valley and founded the Sierra Club. *Stickeen* was written by John Muir and covered his travels and explorations with an exceptional dog named Stickeen. Beautifully written and acted, it related the experience of exploring glaciers in Alaska. John Muir ended his ordeal on a particularly treacherous glacier by seeing such courage and loyalty in his dog that he was moved to understand the connectedness of all living things. His respect for life and love of the wilderness were the dominant themes of his writing and his life. He wrote movingly about these very Sierra Mountains we were encamped in:

> *Wonderful how completely everything in wild nature fits into us, as if truly part and parent of us. The Sun shines not on us but in us. The rivers flow not past, but through us, thrilling, tingling, vibrating every fiber and cell of the substance of our bodies, making them glide and sing. The trees wave and the flowers bloom in our bodies as well as our souls, and every bird song, wind song, and tremendous storm song of the rocks in the heart of the mountains is our song, our very own, and sings our love.*

These 5th-grade children were being immersed in the Yosemite wilderness to create these same experiences, which had transformed John Muir.

I'm glad I took Neil to Yosemite, but next time I'll stay in the mountains and meadows above the valley with a smaller group of quieter people, hoping to invoke the spirit of John Muir's magnificent mountains. I'll never forget those 5 days—the campsite, the children, the teachers, and the parents. But the vision that rests in my mind is of golden aspens shimmering as the wind blows across the faces of the granite mountains, calling me back to the grandeur which is Yosemite.

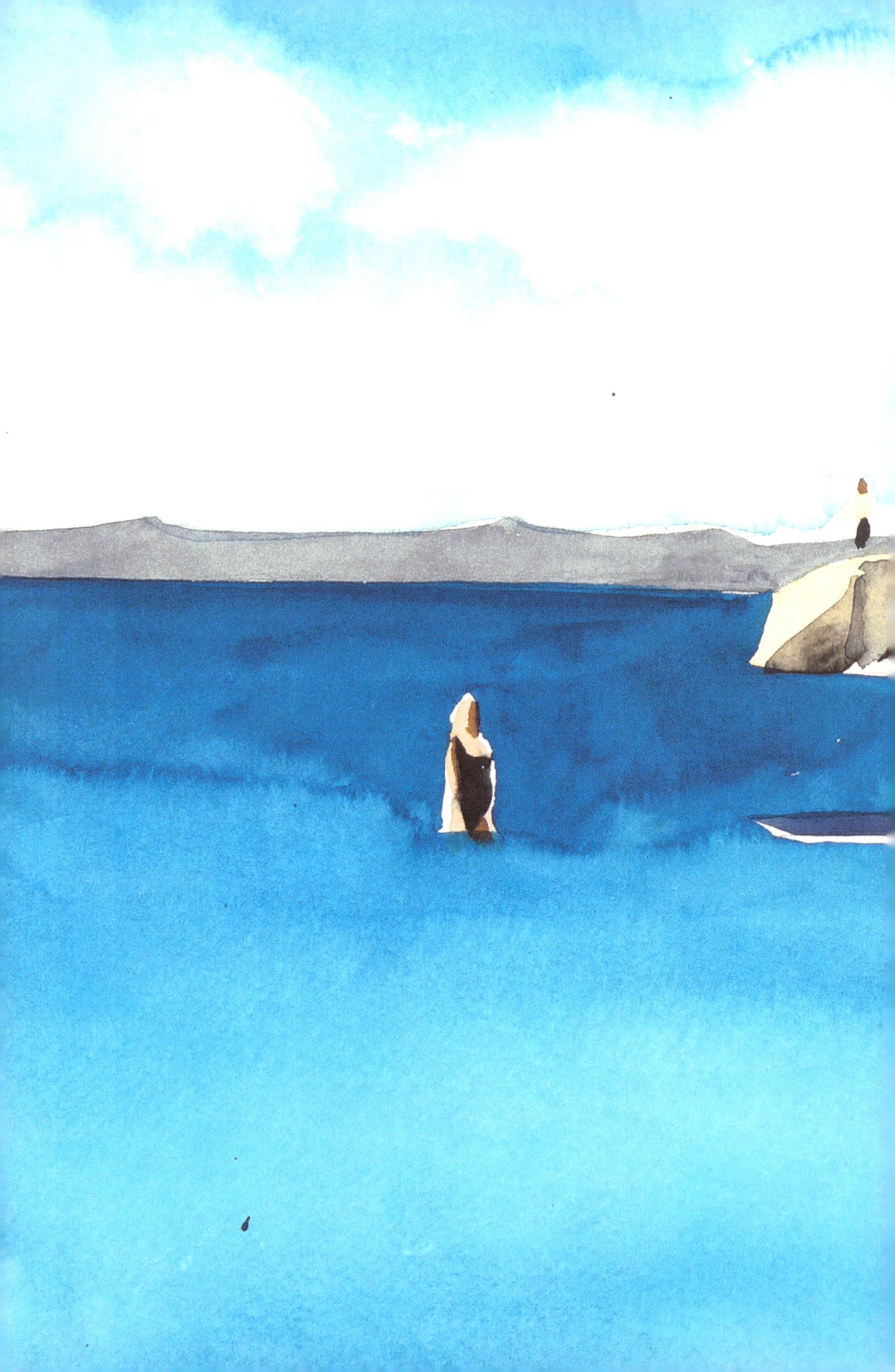

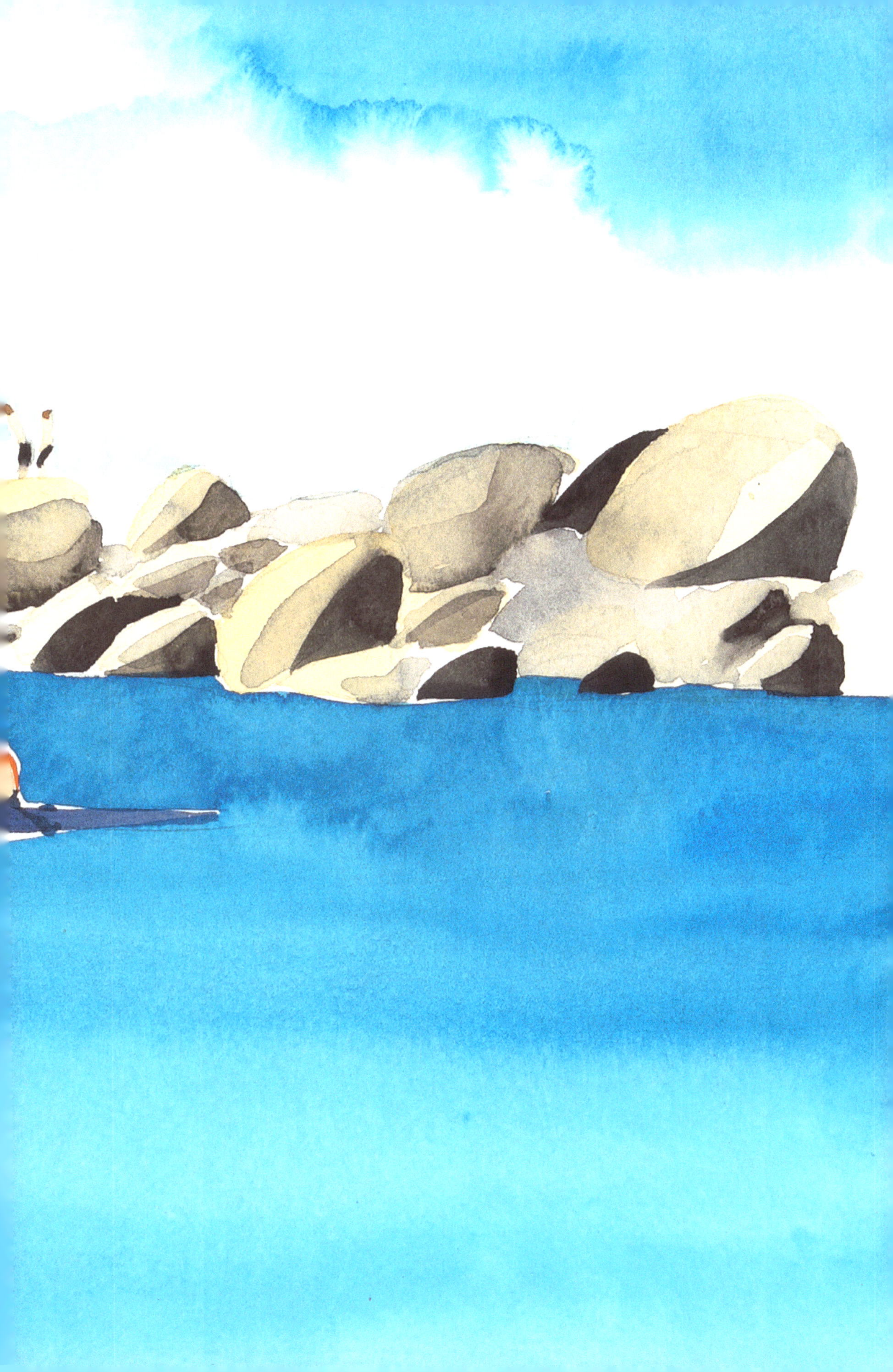

THE DEEP BLUE *Fall 1994*

"You have everything you need," said the gypsy. "You just don't know it yet." She was a modern-day, self-appointed gypsy, and we were on the north shore of Lake Tahoe at a campground near Tahoe City. The tall pine trees were thick and obscured the view of the lake. The air was full of their scent, and the soft breeze rippled through my hair. I had grown it as long as it would grow, and it curled to my waist. My boyfriend's hair only grew just past his shoulders. He had brought me here to camp while his band, *The Loading Zone*, played in a nearby town. The gypsy was the guitar player's girlfriend, her dark hair held back by a bandana that framed large hooped earrings. She dealt tarot cards to foretell my future and assured me that my fate was positive.

I came back to the lake 5 years later under different circumstances. I had married the musician—we had both cut our hair—and we were participating in a conference with several hundred other people to design courses that would be offered at a new university whose curriculum included meditation. We had rented an old estate on the shores of the lake with rock houses scattered amongst the trees and met daily as we watched the fall colors overtake the forests and the breeze off the lake turned cold.

My husband introduced me to the waters of Lake Tahoe with early morning swims off the pier of our rented house (he kept this up through October). The water is a color of blue seen only in the Sierra Sky, so pure you can see 100 feet down in this deeper-than-deep lake. It is circumscribed by tall snowcapped mountains that act as sentinels, protecting the lake from encroaching civilization.

We were on the West Shore in the old-style Tahoe cabins, interspersed with state parks, beaches, and streams of clear melted snow burbling over boulders. Today the cabins remain only in the forests behind the lake. Lakefront property, which can be seen only from boats cruising in close to the shores, is so valuable that only large houses and gated estates, obscured by elaborate landscaping, remain.

We have been to the lake many times since our idyllic stay. We have watched the towns grow and the houses being built. We have taken our babies to the cold waters and initiated them in the rite of passage of the morning swim. The blue remains, and if it's not 100 feet clear it's still very close to it. But the world has discovered Lake Tahoe, and tourists come from all over to swim, boat, ski, cycle, and climb. We try to see beyond the people and the boats, far down into the deep blue pure essence of the Lake. *Lake Tahoe, One Per World* reads a local bumper sticker, which reflects the feelings of all of us who love this lake.

I am still puzzling over the relationship between needing and knowing that the gypsy brought to my attention. Needs are greatest when knowledge is least. As knowledge grows, needs seem to retire into the outer shadows of our lives, still there to haunt on occasion, or to make their presence felt when we are tired or vexed, but knowledge has that wonderful ability to satisfy. Knowledge dispels doubts and quenches our thirst for life, transforming needs into interests and abilities—like a swim in the deep blue of Lake Tahoe. The best way is to boat out beyond the shores, past the sandy bottom, to the deep waters, to the blue that is fathomless—so deep, so pure, so blue (it's what I imagine outer space to be)—and dive in. Everything can be seen: the rocks far below, my red toenails, my family swimming nearby. It is cold but washed with translucence; everything is clear and clean and quiet, absolutely quiet.

Knowledge of inner awareness experienced in silence gives to our minds what a swim in the deep blue gives to our bodies. The gypsy could never have foretold how much self-knowledge would come my way. She couldn't even tell me how many times I would visit the lake with my yet-undeclared love. But she did tell me that my quest for knowledge and my awareness of needs intersected and intertwined in a way I had not realized. I have learned that they balance each other. As my knowledge has grown, my needs have changed from overcoming the insecurities of my youth, to satisfying the concerns of my family, to promoting the happiness of my community, and finally to experiencing the changes that age bestows for better and for worse. My growing awareness continues to wrap itself around my changing needs and transforms them into something that lives within me and fuels my actions.

Lake Tahoe still draws us to her shores—for recreation, family reunions, and the joy of seeing old and new friends. But the real reason we keep returning to the lake is simply the longing for the purity only known with a dive into this deep blue.

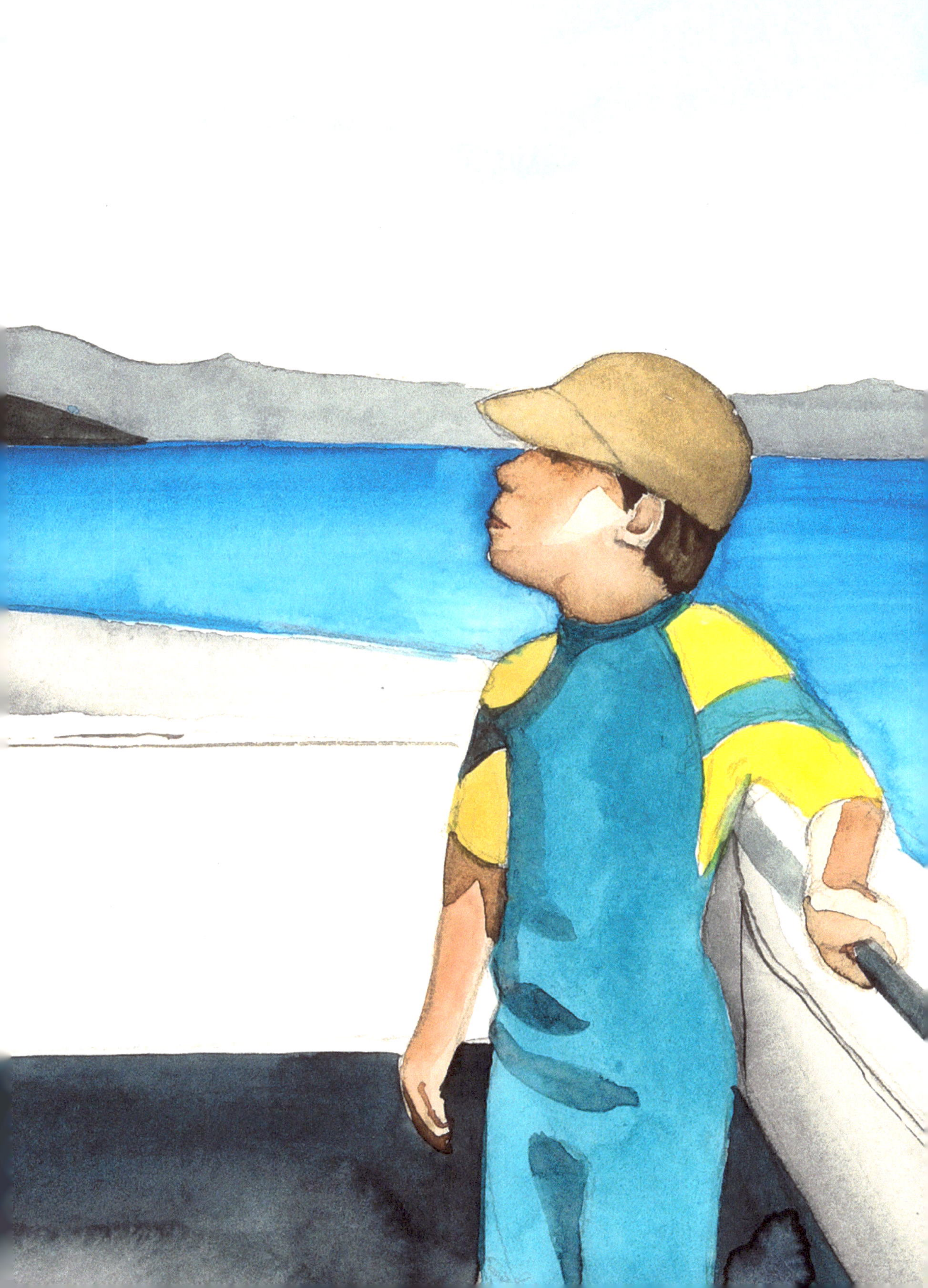

THE RIVER WILD *Summer 1996*

I was praying it would rain. Not because rain was needed; the drought in Northern California had been broken several years ago, and Lake Tahoe was fuller than it had been in years—up 6 feet from the previous summer and within 6 inches of the all-time high. No, I was praying for rain for another reason. We were renting a wonderful cottage in Brockway Springs, a block from the lake, complete with redwood bark siding, a fireplace big enough to walk into, a redwood deck with a peek at the cobalt blue waters, massive granite boulders in the backyard, and its own little guest house. The setting was so idyllic that guests abounded. Along with my husband Paul and our three children (two grown college girls, Elizabeth and Joey, and our 14-year-old son, Neil), our household included my overworked doctor brother, his grown daughter and her boyfriend, and a surprise visit from my nephew Trevor, who had driven 12 hours from Jackson, Wyoming, where he is a white-water river guide on the Snake River. His four-wheel-drive vehicle arrived with two bicycles and a kayak on the roof and a pretty tanned brunette girl, Amy, in the front seat. I shrieked with delight on seeing him because he wasn't expected and because he is a wonderful young man—a tall blond with an amiable face, gentle manners, and a great love of the out-of-doors and adventure.

It didn't take Trevor long to discover that there is a river within an hour and a half of Lake Tahoe with Class 4 and 5 rapids. He proposed we go on a white-water rafting trip—the whole family. Everyone jumped at the opportunity, especially my three children, who were definitely ready for adventure after 10 days in the cabin with their parents, and my brother, who is a white-water rafting aficionado and has rafted the Snake, the Salmon, and the Colorado. My husband of course would never be outdone by my brother, and he too was sending up yelps of enthusiasm. Only I was reticent, or, to tell the truth, I was terrified. The vision of all the people I love dearest in the world engulfed in the violent swirl of the rushing waters of the river haunted me. I knew I couldn't talk them out of it, and I figured that if I went I could at least force my mirthful family to act seriously in the face of danger. The other alternative was, of course, to cancel the trip because of rain: hence my prayers.

It did not rain, at least not in time to cancel the trip. Lest you think me completely spiritually bereft and without influence with the Almighty, I will tell you straightaway that all who went on the trip (my entire family and my brother in one boat, Trevor in his kayak, and pretty Amy in another boat) finished the trip alive and able to walk up the hill away from the final embankment. However, the 17-mile ride down the middle fork of the American River was an experience I won't soon forget.

White-water rafting is rated according to the difficulty and danger of the rapids encountered. A river can have many levels of rapids, from Class 2—easy, to Class 3—exciting, to Class 4—difficult, to Class 5—most difficult. This river had quite a few Class-4 rapids and one Class 5 as well as many Class 3 and 2 sections. It didn't sound like something I would be interested in!

Our trip began in the parking lot of a McDonald's in Auburn, California, where we were meeting our rafting company. It turned out there were other rafters as well—milling around, applying sunscreen, and making jokes. One woman was jauntily attired with nylon shorts, a tank-style bathing suit, a bandana tied around her neck, a nylon baseball cap, aqua boots, and a waterproof watch, as well as sunglasses on a cord. She came up to me as I leaned against our car with a dejected and apprehensive look on my face. "Your first trip?" she inquired. "Yes," I confessed, eager to express my fears. "I don't know what I am doing here. I'm scared to death and I don't want to go, but my family dragged me here." (Actually my nephew was being extremely solicitous, having made all the arrangements himself and continuously assuring me that it was a very good outfit we were going with, that I could do it, and he would watch out for us, etc.) The lady told me she was a kayaker too, but she used inflatable kayaks and was investigating the river to see if she could kayak here later in the summer. She told me not to be scared—that it would be good for me and I would feel I had really accomplished something by the end of the trip.

We rode in a van along a road on the side of a mountain, looking down into a deep ravine with a tiny ribbon at its bottom that was our river. As we wound our way down I couldn't help but admire the terrain. We were passing the foothills of the Sierras, forested with wide spreading oaks, flowered with yellow sage, and dotted with the taller spruce and pines that dominate the higher areas around Lake Tahoe. Our embarkation point was just yards away from the dam that holds the melted snows of the entire Desolation Wilderness area (the mountains to the west of Lake Tahoe), letting the water out from its base and creating an ice-cold river with waters that warm to about 50 degrees in the shallowest areas.

We were issued faded orange life vests with a slightly mildewed smell, white helmets with tight chin straps that were extremely unflattering, and paddles with long handles. Our guide, Eric, gave us our introductory lecture. Basically, we were to follow his instructions or the raft would flip. If we fell out we were to go down the river feet first and grab the paddles that would be extended by the rafters still in the boats or in dire emergencies grab the lifeline that the guide would throw out. Very encouraging. Once we were launched in the raft, Eric gave us our paddle commands: Easy Forward, Forward, Fast Forward, Back Paddle, Turn Left, Turn Right (opposite sides of the raft paddling in different directions, as in a canoe), Highside Left, Highside Right (those seated on one side of the raft must climb atop those seated on the other side of the raft to create a tilt of the entire boat), and Get Down (used only for the most difficult rapids to prevent anything striking the sides of the chute that would create a ricochet of the boat on the hard granite rocks). Well, I paid real close attention to these commands and am happy to say that so did my family. We dutifully paddled very hard in those first gentle rolls. My brother Walter and my husband Paul sat in the front, my daughter Elizabeth and I sat in the next row, and Neil and Johanna sat in the third row, with Eric the Great at the rear, sitting high with his paddle, which he used like a rudder to steer the raft. We were instructed to sit on the inflated outer edge of the boat and put our feet in slots on the bottom to secure ourselves (Oh, Dear). The rapids alternated with calm stretches of easy-flowing water, and with each roll I looked to my right (the front was just too scary), paddle held with military alertness, awaiting the commands.

After what I realize now are easy rapids, our guide instructed us to pull over into an eddy, get out of the raft, climb a hill, and view the next rapid. This was the only Class 5 rapid on the trip. I was the last to walk up the trail, and my daughters had doubled back with apprehensive looks on their faces. "Mom, you can walk around this one. I don't think you'll want to do it." I would have felt better if they had said "we don't want to do it." It took my breath away to look down on the rapid called Tunnel Chute, where the river narrowed to about 12 feet wide with granite cliffs on either side and descended 25 feet over about 25 yards in a roar of white water to a pool of swirling water feeding into a tunnel that was cut through the mountain. Everyone stared, trying to imagine themselves in a raft in that chute and one by one came up with some expression of bravura to demonstrate their courage and commit themselves to this crazy act. Of course my family were amongst the jubilant novices raising their voices in defiance of common sense. I swallowed my fear, banished my thoughts, and marched toward the raft to their evident approval: "Alright, Mom!" We paddled out to the middle of the river, and our guide called the commands to position us to take the chute. This was the critical moment because the angle of entrance was the only thing we had control of; once we were in the chute the river was in total control. I have to say my unruly family was very alert, uncharacteristically quiet, completely efficient, and perfectly coherent. We made a perfect run, completely doused in the icy waters, exhilarated and amazed as we emerged out of the other side of the tunnel to look back and watch Trevor in his kayak, rolling under the water and back up again. It was only at the end of the trip that he told us that he took the entire rapid upside down in his kayak. Ah, intrepid youth!

After Tunnel Chute we were confident that we could handle anything, and the next few rapids did seem easy although they involved more technical maneuvering. Lunch was a welcome break on the side of the river under a large tree. My prayers were finally answered as we spread the mayonnaise on our sandwiches and a generous downpour of rain accompanied the loud thunder and flashing lightning. But guess what? I was unfazed. The test on the river made me impervious to my ordinary caution. I didn't even shiver as I downed my lemonade and dipped my soggy chips.

The rain stopped and the clouds cleared just as we got back in the rafts and started a slow float down the river. Ahead of us a foggy mist rose from the river to a height of 15 feet, creating low-lying clouds that engulfed the rafts in front of us in a dreamy disappearing act while hundreds of double-winged dragon flies floated above. It could have been a scene from Jurassic Park. On either side of the river the banks rose in beautiful high mountains, forested with green trees and crowned with bright blue skies. The sun began to beat down on us, and we realized we were fortunate to have had a morning of cool temperatures and overcast skies. We couldn't resist the occasional dip in the river, although 30 seconds seemed to be the maximum we could stay in and our reentry was awkward and undignified, being dragged up and across the raft by the tops of our life jackets.

Occasionally we would see deserted river vehicles on the rocky shores of the river, with flotation cylinders and random riggings going in every direction and a rusty propeller jutting out. These looked like something out of the movie Waterworld, but they are apparently used for gold mining in the river. This is California gold rush territory, and the river still hides a reasonable amount of gold.

We paddled up to another group of rafters, held in rapt attention by a small water snake on the side of a tree. "You'd better look out," my brother cried. "That looks like the Amazonian Water Viper—it can jump 20 feet in the air." "Yeah," my husband chimed in. "And it can spew venom all the way across a river." The rafters' paddles carried them back and away from the little snake so quickly that they didn't have time to ponder how a creature from the Amazon could be in Northern California, how any snake could jump 20 feet in the air or spray venom across a river, or why another group of rafters would be laughing in front of their vision of menace. Oh Well… my brothers and my husband are very naughty men, but their time of reckoning was at hand. We had reached the Class 6 rapid, illegal to even attempt, which meant that we had to portage the raft around it.

The rafts we used were self-bailing, which means they had a hard bottom loosely strung to the inflatable sides. This made them heavier than the usual raft, weighing over 200 pounds. Eric instructed Paul and Walter to stand at the front and center and to heave the raft above their heads and follow the narrow rocky trail around the roaring rapid. Eric was in the rear of this portage crew. The only trouble was that Paul at 6'5" and Walter at 6'4" bore the brunt of the weight and inevitably came to rest the raft on their heads, making their necks strain and their gait wobble. I honestly think that was the most dangerous moment of the trip—an unsteady march along the cliff side, teetering over huge granite rocks awash with the wildest waters I have ever seen. Fortunately it was a short trip to the cove at the base of the rapids, where we once again "put in" and resumed our trip. The boys were temporarily subdued but regained their spirits with loud faux commands for paddling through calm waters: "Und stroke, und stroke," etc.

We still had to pass through a series of Class 4 rapids with names like Texas Chain Saw Mama, Parallel Parking, and Final Exam. After pulling into a gentle eddy, we walked up a steep hill to our final embankment and rejoined the rest of the people who were rafting with our company. I noticed right away that my friend, the jaunty lady, was walking around with one of her aqua boots missing, her hat and glasses also gone. She bore a dazed and weary expression. "Did it go alright for you?" I asked, feeling some concern. "Our guide called the wrong command on the Texas Chain Saw rapid," she answered, "and I was thrown from the boat. I spent what seemed like forever under the water and began swallowing water; I almost drowned." "How terrible!" I replied. "Yeah, I burst into tears when they finally hauled me into the boat. You know, if it had been my mistake, it would have been easier to take."

Later that afternoon I happened upon her raft-mates as we all inspected photographs (taken by a professional photographer) of each of our rafts going down Tunnel Chute. As we excitedly looked at ourselves, mouths agape, roaring through the white water, I asked them about the near drowning in their raft. "Oh come on," one woman said, "she was under 3 seconds at the most. Several of us went in; it was no big deal." I guess fear had overtaken this woman. I could feel quite a bit of sympathy for her because fear had been nipping at my heels all through that day. I realized I had outrun it when I heard myself saying to Eric, "So next summer we'll call you and we'll bring my other brother too—you'll love him—and we can go up to Oregon and do that overnight on the Klamath River you were telling us about."

Now that I am home I am not at all sure I will go back to white-water rafting. Hiking seems more appropriate for someone like me—fifty, female, and fearful—but over and beyond the sheer fun of the wild ride down that river, it felt really good to rise above my apprehensions, reservations, wariness, doubt, anxieties, worry, and discomfort and just go with the flow!

ON THE WAY TO MONTANA *Summer 1998*

Pleasantville, Iowa is one of those towns with a builder's supply store made out of corrugated metal, a steakhouse made of brick with no windows, and a retirement living area set in pretty rolling hills. The big barns at the edge of town, collapsing from within, contrasted with the neat tract homes we viewed through chain-link fences. "I could never live in a town like this," my husband declared as we passed through. "I could," I said, not knowing if I was telling the truth. Pleasantville is only 30 miles from Des Moines, which despite being our state capital was not our destination. No, we were headed west, hankering for open sky and large stretches of land.

"Passing through" is a great experience. Skimming someone else's reality, forming easy opinions and likes and dislikes: propriety with no responsibility. We always dress casually, more casually than we live, shorts and jeans and t-shirts. We eat ice cream and soda and listen to what we used to call soul music, slapping our legs and bouncing in our seats, oblivious to the fact that we are now in our fifties and not young, firm, and rebellious anymore. But road trips make people feel free, and the road trip West is the one necessary American experience. As the wonders of the West begin to open up to the traveler, everyone has the same experience of relief, disbelief, and awe.

Our 16-year-old son was driving us through South Dakota just days after getting his driver's license. In fact that was the ostensible reason for the trip; we had to go to California so we thought we'd give him unlimited driving experience. One thing led to another—South Dakota led to Montana and Flathead Lake, which led to Coeur d'Alene, Idaho, then to the Columbia River Gorge in Northern Oregon, right on to the Redwoods in Northern California, which logically led to the San Francisco Bay Area, where we needed to go in the first place.

South Dakota doesn't like animal activists. They claim to need meat and fur for their "livelihood," according to the billboards we encountered on first passing into the state. Indeed the wonders of the West do begin at the border between Iowa and South Dakota with a "scenic overlook," which is a road that wanders off the highway and up a hill with a small tower perched on it. It was closed when we drove by, but as we wound our way out of the bluffs onto the plains we realized that it was probably possible to see for hundreds of miles across the prairie. We connected to Interstate 90 and drove to the Missouri River, where the Lewis and Clark Memorial Bridge and Rest Stop commemorates the intrepid corps of explorers who made their way upstream, each man eating 9 pounds of meat a day, looking for the headwaters of the river and a water route across the continent to the Pacific. Everything is named for Lewis and Clark here, and God knows they deserve it. But I'd like to see a little more in the way of appreciation for Sacagawea, the Indian girl who helped them navigate their dangerous journey. She did the same trip with a baby!

The plains stretched out for hundreds of miles behind us and a glimpse of the Black Hills of South Dakota looked as if they had been pinched up heavenward and the dark silhouette of the first hills in probably thousands of miles was startling.

We stayed in Spearfish, an idyllic town in the mouth of a beautiful canyon next to a clear rushing stream. Spearfish has a small college, a community theater, and a big city park next to the stream. As fanciful a house as any I have ever seen is there, set behind a 10-foot-high hedge in a garden of colorful perennials with porches on several sides; one porch is draped in lace curtains even though it is outside. Dormer windows peek out over a wood-shingled roof, and there is a feeling everywhere of pleasant self-satisfaction. This feeling, in fact, pervades the little city. We stayed in The Cottonwood Lodge, which is made of logs and features a great room that must be 30 feet high, with an amazing stone fireplace. An interior courtyard with swings and drooping trees has a soft breeze blowing persistently through it.

What was puzzling is that although it was July 3, only two other guests were there. To account for this, I made up a story: A man approaching his forties decided it was time to realize his dreams and took his savings—maybe he was a lawyer or had made money in the stock market or inherited a nest egg—and carefully built a lodge, selecting all the stones from the surrounding mountains for the fireplace and hearth and buying his logs, which were extra large, from Canada. Every door latch was of the highest quality, and all the furnishings were the tasteful Western style, interspersed with Western antiques—wagon wheels and implements. Within the lodge was a small pub with pictures on walls of a motorcycle club called The Hamsters—a sort of spoof on the tough motorcycle gangs. These guys, from the look of their pictures on the walls of the pub, were mainly amiable professional people, proving a point to themselves. Men and the occasional go-along gal were dressed in jeans and identical shirts, looking relaxed, if a bit scruffy. I think the owner lost his lodge as a result of a bitter divorce—or maybe he went too far with his dream, maybe he got a terrible illness, maybe he just had to send his kids to college and couldn't subsidize his dream any longer. At any rate the lodge was changing ownership and evinced a sad feeling despite the beautiful construction.

Outside of Spearfish we entered Wyoming. We passed by Devil's Tower and took time to circumambulate the tall odd granite structure before heading north for Montana.

The fourth biggest state spreads from east to west across high plains, rising into the Bitterroot and Mission mountain ranges. Big valleys stretch between peaks—the biggest valleys in the world, I think. They dwarf everything else in the landscape and make something as small as a person seem insignificant. We were headed for Big Sky—although everything in Montana has a big sky—for the Fourth of July. We stayed on the Gallatin River in a log cabin and spent the evening listening to local musicians play at a community hoedown capped by fireworks.

The next day we made our way north, through more beautiful valleys, into and out of Indian reservations, to Flathead Lake. We had rented another log cabin right on Flathead Lake, which we had come to evaluate in comparison to Lake Tahoe, our favorite lake in the known universe. Flathead Lake is the largest freshwater lake west of the Mississippi River. It is bordered on the east by the Mission and Swan mountains and on the west by the Blackfoot Mountain Range. The north and south borders of the lake are large expansive valleys with wide rivers feeding into and out of the lake. Flathead Lake is a flow-through lake, which means that water that goes in through the rivers (mainly various forks of the Flathead River, and the Swan River) comes out after a few years. One of the hazards of the lake is the floating logs, which are part of the rivers' contributions to the lake. Compared to the size of the lake, there are not many boats, and the lake has many fingers and coves—many miles of lakefront—some of which is covered with beautiful cherry orchards.

Of the nearby towns that cater to tourists, the biggest is Kalispell, populated by 18,000 people and 10 miles north of the lake. This is where my husband's uncle lives, and part of our itinerary was to see all of our relatives who live in the West.

Uncle Hal is a legend in the Fauerso family. Ruggedly handsome, he is the youngest of six children and has done things as varied as drive logging trucks before there were interstate highways, fight with Carson's Raiders in World War II, and model for different industrial products. He had sold real estate around Flathead Lake for the past 20 years, using his naturally effusive personality to make his mark in the area. The Flathead Lake setting is so idyllic that one is tempted to see it as a place where humans can escape the rough part of our destiny—the tragedy, difficulties, and surprises that fate has in store for most of us. Hal's story underscores the futility of these hopes. His youngest son, Steve, was involved in a one-car accident when he was 19. He was asleep in the backseat of a VW Bug late at night when the driver plowed into a brick wall. The guys in the front seat were bunged up but basically unharmed. Steve's vertebrae were crushed, and he was left a quadriplegic. Through perseverance he has been able to reclaim the use of his arms and hands. Hal's daughter, Judy, a few years older than Steve, also lives in the area. Her husband is the game warden for the county, and she has an adopted African-American son named Nathan.

The Montana Fauersos have carved interesting lives for themselves. Steve owns a restaurant and is married to a beautiful woman who is a member of the Indian tribe that owns the reservation south of the lake. She is blond and fair, due to her English mother, but has a sense of resignation and immediacy about her. Judy lives on 60 beautiful acres with her husband and son and five dogs, three horses, a donkey, and a dozen or so cattle.

Connecting with the Montana Fauersos proved to be a dance of obtuse communications and a lesson for me on why my husband is so weird! It is not for these people to say "I would really like to see you. Come over on Thursday at 3 and I'll show you around and then we can meet the others at 7 for dinner in Lakeside." Actually, in my family that would have been said 6 months before the event, and woe to the person who changed any of the details. But in this family, options are left open until just before any impending event, with phrases like "I don't want to interfere with your vacation," or "We don't want to tell you what to do," or "You could come over any time, if you want." It took no fewer than eight telephone calls to "touch base" before a time and place were set up to have dinner. This helped me understand why my husband always has to call people to set up another time to call them to make a time for a meeting!

The much-discussed dinner took place at a wonderful old restaurant on the north shore of the lake. Its piano bar featured an elderly black lady pianist who played the blues and old standards—her hands with large knuckles spread wide across the keyboard. She was a seasoned pro who humored Hal as he stood to sing several of his old favorites. Paul sat down with her to play a duet of "Summertime" that brought the house down. Hal was in his element that night, and it is how we will always remember him. A year later he was dead from a fatal heart attack, and when we returned for his memorial, the blues lady was gone as well.

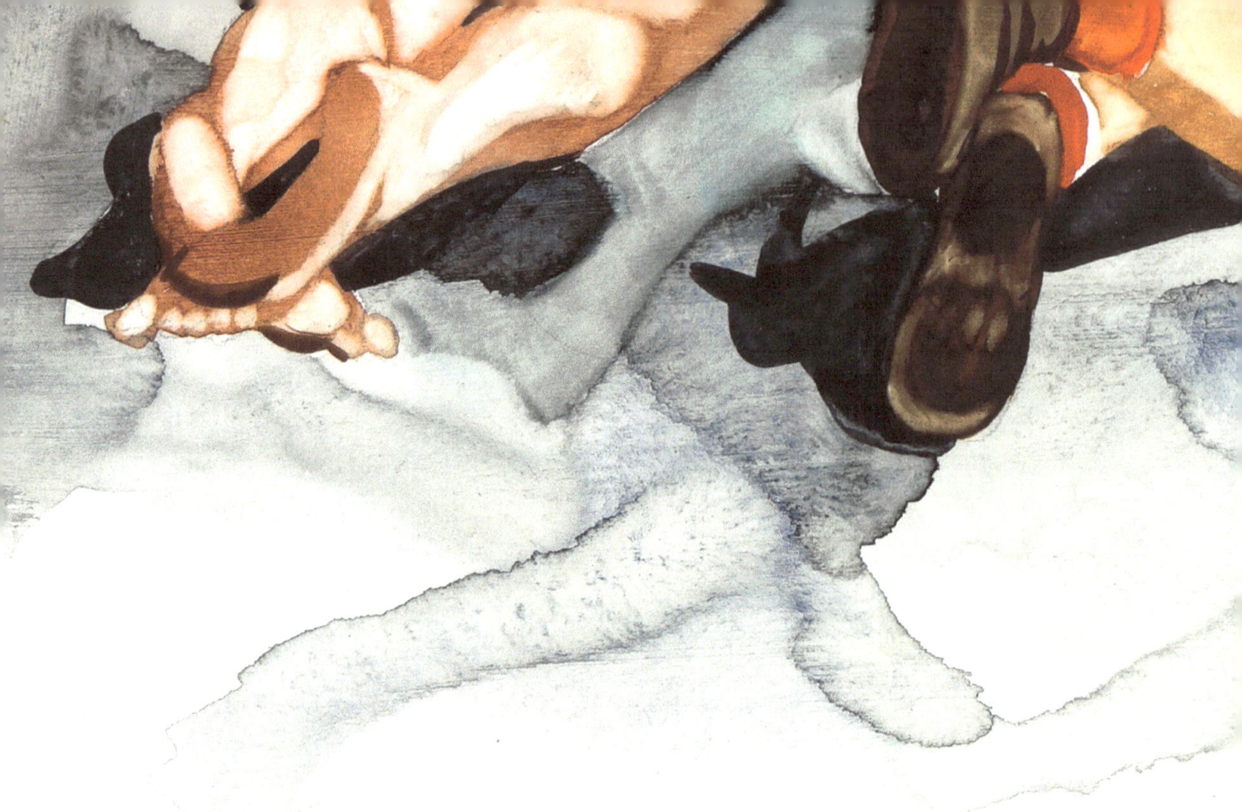

FAMILY REUNION

Summer 1993

Get on the plane, take the train, pack the car, it's time to see your families again. As the holiday season gets underway, many families come together for their annual or biannual meetings. Family reunions are making a comeback in American life, aided by instant communication systems and efficient modes of travel. And it is not only the holidays that afford this challenging undertaking. The ritual of the gathering of members of tribes, known as the family reunion, can take place at any time all across America. The experience itself presents challenges and rewards that are often overlooked in the tumult of the moment. This summer my family collected itself in San Francisco just after my husband's family had collected itself in Oregon. We attended the San Francisco reunion, watched several hours of videotape of the Oregon reunion, and various themes began to emerge that I can't help but think must be played out in family festivities across our nation.

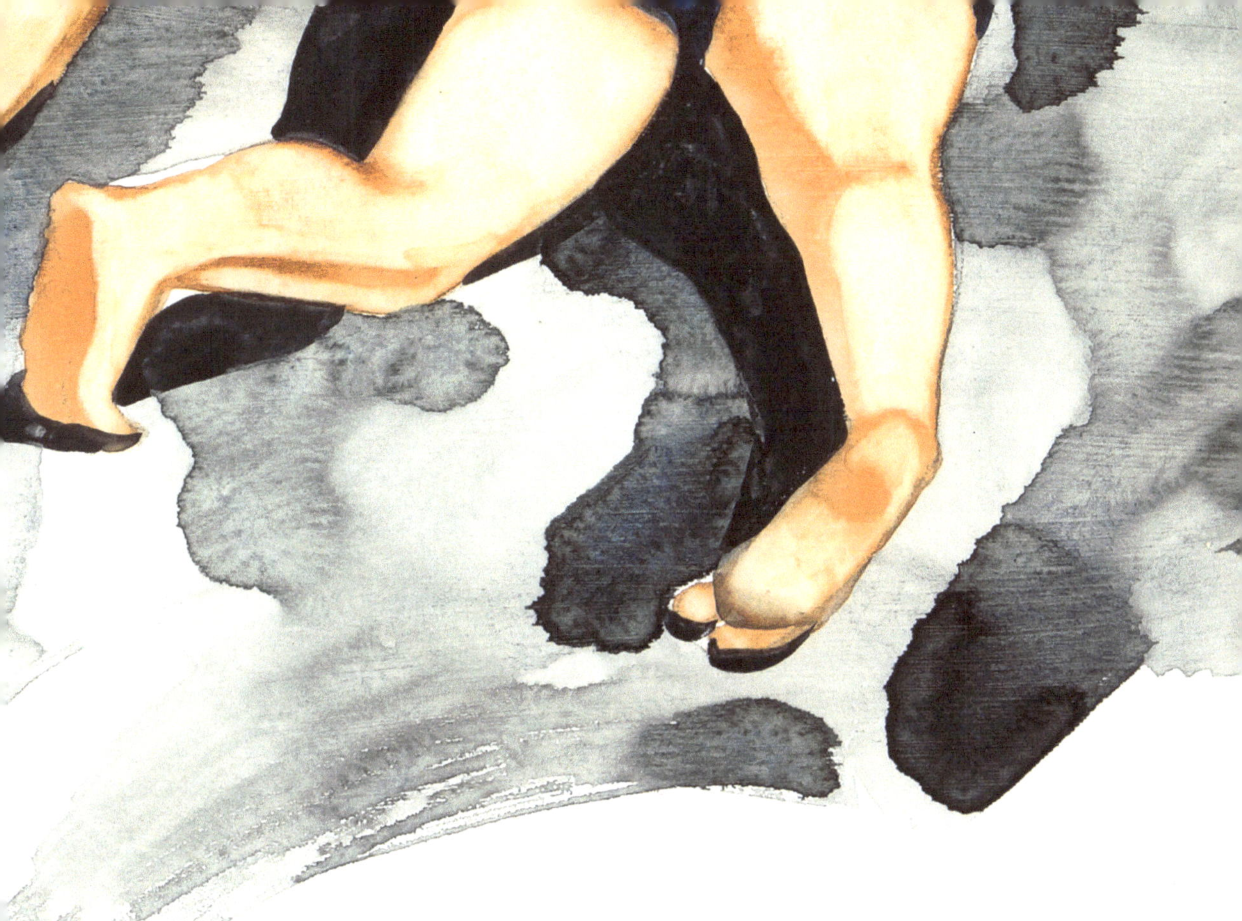

Family gatherings are by their nature chaotic, noisy affairs with cousins confronting each other across the seas of their lives and siblings connecting on a bed of memories and past patterns of relating. My family gathering included all three of my brothers, their wives and children, my own husband and three children, my mother, and the wife and two babies of one of my nephews.

My family sports lots of pairs. We have two Willards, two Walters, two Sebastians, a Josie and a Joey, and the unlikely doubling of two Agnes Bains—my mother, the matriarch of this clan, and the young wife of one of my nephews and the mother of my mother's only great grandchildren. Does this sound confusing? It's actually an intelligence test in disguise, sorting out these varied relationships.

Family reunions are encouraging and discouraging at the same time. One feels secure to belong to a group of people, proud to be related to certain ones, a little reluctant to be related to others. Every family has its tragedies and triumphs. In my own family, this is particularly poignant for me—my oldest brother, a writer and my mentor, has suffered from a debilitating mental illness for over 25 years. In spite of this, his gentle nature and astute mind shine through the symptoms of his illness. This summer he witnessed our clan converge on the park near his home in Marin County, California. He sat and watched as his beautiful grand-babies, with golden curls circling their faces like halos, greeted his mother, brothers, and sons for the first time.

All families have traits that become obvious as their group collects. In our family, the men are tall. They play basketball as a matter of course, and that Sunday in Marin County the boys and men collected on the outdoor B-ball court with the bright blue sky above them. Sebastian, aged two, bounced on the sidelines as he watched 7-year-old Mikey brave the friendly combat with his 6'6" father and his uncles and cousins of various heights between his own and his father's. Even my oldest brother panted his way through the game, collapsing into a heap at the end as the littlest children climbed on him, oblivious of his exhaustion.

Along with basketball, my family excels at conversation. Members of my family settle around a restaurant table with a sense of anticipation, knowing that other diners will be either bothered or amused by the uproarious laughter coming from that table. My husband, the raconteur of the family, will have many anecdotes to report while my brothers embellish and interpret the witty climaxes to the stories—laying their verbal challenges like trumpets announcing the beginning of a joust. The dueling that ensues is not for the fainthearted, and we have learned who will be the players and who will be the spectators. My mother, the referee, brings closure to topics—moving the evening along whether it means ordering the food, changing the subject, or declaring a winner. As my husband is fond of saying, "When Agnes lays it down, it stays down!"

We have teachers, writers, artists, a doctor, MBAs, salespeople, meditators, fishermen, tennis champions, good cooks, and great enjoyers of food. There are those who are quiet and those who are loud—the leaders and the followers, the active and the settled—but all of us feel close to each other, like belonging to a private club whose membership requirement is to enjoy each other's company. As you can imagine, the number of jokes that have accumulated over the years is encyclopedic. One of my favorites is my younger brother's imitation of his math teacher from the eighth grade—Mr. Crawford— who speaks out of only one side of his mouth as he explains that what he is teaching is not exactly math but that it is a lot like math. The repetition of certain jokes and routines is part of our family rituals and almost always gets us laughing. It is our way of coping; no matter what has happened, we are able to find the comfortable path that humor makes to the happier side of our natures, where love and intimacy emerge.

The Oregon reunion had a casual, outdoorsy feel to it. This group of Fauersos (a name unique to my husband's family, changed from the overused Nielsen in Denmark nearly 100 years ago) is at home in the mountains and woods: burly men in plaid flannel shirts and capable-looking women. Many were outgoing, bridging the gaps that time had chiseled between the cousins and aunts and uncles. A bright group of children bounced in and out of the video, and one we noticed in particular, with a round face crowned by a blond buzz cut, reminded us of pictures of my husband as a lad.

Engineering runs strongly in this family. My father-in-law was a chief engineer for Standard Oil before he retired, and his father was the county engineer in his area of Oregon. Uncle Hal, a friendly bear of a man, displayed an old photograph of a stunning bridge uniting two promontories across a dizzyingly deep ravine that Grandpa Chris Fauerso designed and built years ago.

Music and music appreciation also hold strong interests among the Fauersos. An encounter with the West-Coast Fauersos always brings

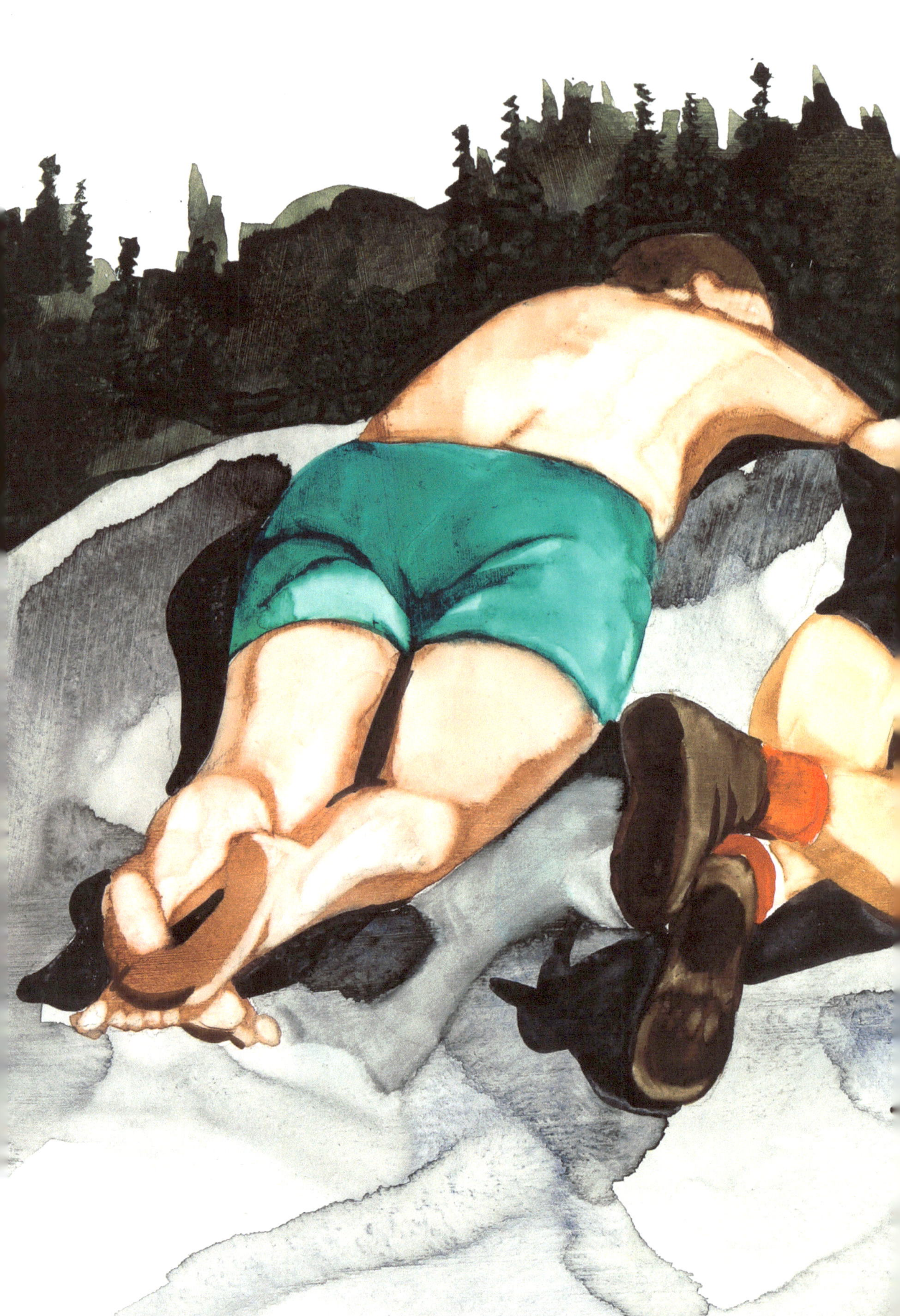

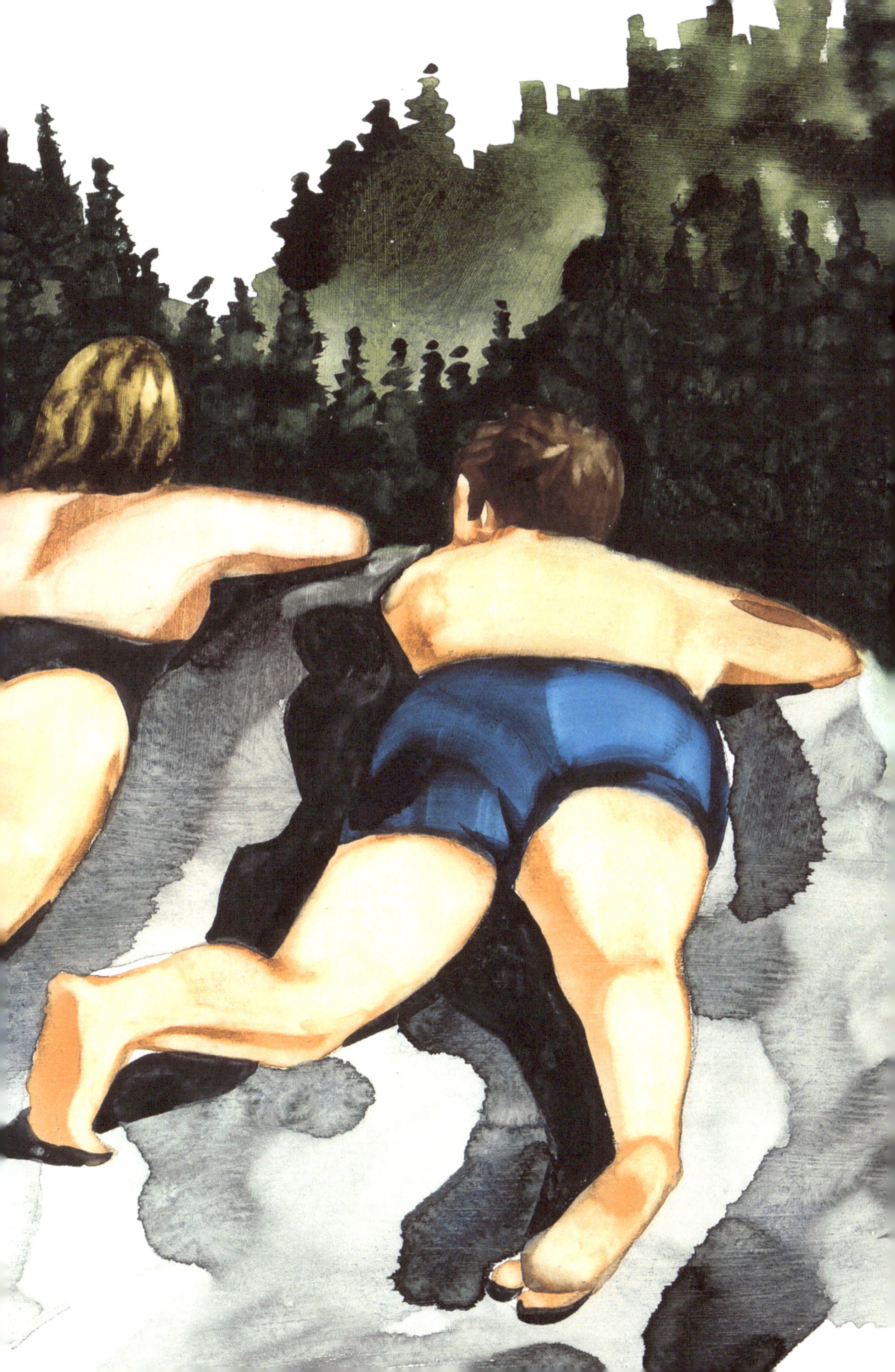

an energetic exchange of recent musical discoveries and listening sessions dedicated to old favorites. Even the elders will occasionally jump from their seats to render a unique (and often hilarious) interpretation of dance to the lively musical rhythms.

The Fauersos, full of good humor and earthy jokes, also exhibit forbearance and loyalty. Our cousin Steve, as noted above, is a member of our generation who was injured in a car accident at 19 and has been a quadriplegic ever since. He is a handsome man with several successful businesses who is very cherished by his family. His father drove from Montana to San Diego to bring his son's mother to the reunion.

I know three other families who attended reunions this summer, and everywhere I go I see groups of people with likenesses echoing off of each other in noisy confusion. As Thomas Hardy, the English novelist, wrote,

I am the family face;
Flesh perishes, I live on,
Projecting trait and trace
Through time to times anon,
And leaping from place to place
Over Oblivion.

With an eye to enjoying this "family face," I'm preparing to meet my own clan on the Texas coast next year, and to meet all those Fauersos in Solvang, California in 2 years. It won't be long before our kids have their own families and our family reunion will mean seeing our children and grandchildren. I expect our roles to change as we become the keepers of the family traditions—passing on the lore from the Bains and Fauersos, encouraging the new generation of parents, and taking our place as the elders of the clan who relinquish the reins of control and relish the freedom of wisdom.

We can thank our parents for giving us the gift of family and our children for giving us the future of family. But we can thank the family reunion for extending our sense of who our family is and giving us the opportunity to get to know them. As you prepare to meet your extended families this holiday season, don't sigh with reluctance. It will most likely be just the thing you need to reconnect with your long-lost relatives and take note of your own unique tribal traits.

URBAN RENEWAL

Fall 1995

I live in a rural community in Southeast Iowa, and I use the city in the same way that city people use the country, but in reverse. I have plenty of peace and quiet here, and I go to the city for excitement and stimulation. This summer found me leaving my peaceful habitat and escorting my two college-age daughters to New York City. My friends had set up house in New Jersey, an hour from NYC, and we went to visit them. We flew into the Newark airport and enjoyed a relaxed evening in a country-like setting and a restful night's sleep. The next morning we boarded the commuter train to NYC. As we passed through the New Jersey countryside we encountered familiar sights: villages with shops and apartment complexes, city parks with baseball diamonds, and residential areas with two-story clapboard houses and green sloped yards that butted up to one another. At the Hoboken, New Jersey station we descended a flight of concrete stairs amidst a stream of purposeful people, fed a dollar into a machine, passed through the turnstile, and stepped onto the Path Train, which passes under the Hudson River through a long, dark tunnel. Loud clanging noises accompanied the jolts as the train lunged through the darkness. The dingy compartment enclosed a variety of people—businessmen in suits with their attaché cases glanced occasionally at the young men dressed in athletic clothing, and poor people hugged tattered bags of possessions while the well-dressed middle-aged women read their books.

The train stopped at 32nd Street and 6th Avenue, and we emerged to an entirely new world. Tall buildings cut a pattern in the skyscape as we glanced upward. The first thing I saw was a large billboard on the front of a building the size of a city block. It read "The World's Largest Store, Macy's." We crossed the street and began walking briskly with no idea where we were headed, flanked by buildings 40 stories high with car horns echoing off the cement sidewalks and pedestrians rushing past us.

In an instant one of my daughters recognized a young man on the street. "Jason!" she called out in astonishment. Two friends from her college in Texas stood before us, their friendly faces contradicting the assumption that we were in a sea of strangers. It was a nice welcome to New York City and gave us confidence to at least ask directions, turn 180 degrees around, and hail a cab. We intended to go the Metropolitan Museum of Art, one of the city's biggest tourist attractions.

We endured a jerky ride through beautiful Central Park, the 840-acre expanse of lush vegetation in the very heart of the city enjoyed by bicyclers, rollerbladers, joggers, and children alike. We emerged on the East Side, the upscale area where Madison Avenue's apparel shops and Park Avenue's elegant high-rises run parallel to Fifth Avenue and the Metropolitan Museum rises majestically above the street. Its massive neoclassical entrance was thronged with people coming and going and eating hotdogs purchased from the vendors positioned on the formal terraces. The Met is bordered at the back by Central Park.

We met a friend, a sometime NYC native, and being hungry, made our way to the cafeteria, determined not to spend a fortune. I gulped at the 52-dollar total for lunch for four of us and the 7-dollar per person "suggested" admission price. This donation, however, proved to be a bargain. The museum is a magnificent place, from its large vaulted entry to its quiet indoor glass-walled gardens. The exhibition rooms are many, varied, well lit, and utterly irresistible, housing more than 3.3 million works of ancient, medieval, classical, and modern art.

We were drawn to the suite of rooms that housed the French Impressionist painters. The collection is sumptuous, with rooms full of Cezanne's still-lifes, Monet's serene landscapes, Renoir's ravishing domestic scenes, Degas' dancers, and Van Gogh's turbulent self-portraits. My daughters, both art students, were enraptured and lost to the stirring visions, any of which could inhabit our imaginations for days. We wandered the rooms and observed the crowds of ethnically and culturally diverse people: urban young people with combat boots and tattoos showing under their undershirts, perky middle-aged couples in sneakers and Bermuda shorts, droopy-looking hippies with long skirts, affluent matrons at the information booths and shops, and young couples torn between the exhibits and their own passionate embraces. We reluctantly left to catch the train back to New Jersey before dusk.

As we exited the front of the building and climbed down the many stairs to the street, we heard cries in the distance amid the dull, persistent roar of the traffic. Walking down the street we passed a young woman who was yelling into the phone at a public phone booth, "I never said that to you, you're lying." By this time I felt out of place, unprepared for the onslaught of sounds, impressions, and feelings the city dishes out. I had not developed the protective barrier necessary for life in this intense urban world. I was still looking into people's eyes, smiling at strangers, and speaking in a way that revealed my unfamiliarity with the city. My daughters, however, were intrigued and ready to take the city on. They wanted to stay overnight, with friends of theirs. I said "Yes" to one and "No" to the other; I needed a companion for the train ride back to New Jersey.

We met up again the next afternoon at a restaurant, an Italian trattoria near Times Square where Broadway at 42nd Street intersects Seventh Avenue. The broad avenue separates, forming a V pattern accentuated by a triangular skyscraper, The Times Building, with an enormous neon billboard. If you've ever watched TV on New Year's Eve you've seen this billboard signaling in the New Year with its 14,800 electric lights. At around 7:30 PM, theater-going pedestrians throng the streets and excitement fills the air as the lights on the theater marquees are lit. Many choices present themselves, from long-running Broadway hits like *Phantom of the Opera* and *Les Miserables* to revivals like *Showboat* and *Damn Yankees* to premiers like Trevor Nunn's *Arcadia*. We chose a revival of a period piece called The Heiress, based on the William James story *Washington Square*.

Anticipation showed on the faces of the crowd entering the beautiful Cort Theater, built in the old style in 1912, with balconies and box seats. It was home to the Merv Griffin Show from 1969 to 1974. Restored to legitimacy after that, it featured 1,920 performances of Doug Henning's hit The Magic Show. The Heiress was good, and we enjoyed it, but most of all we enjoyed the spectacle and ritual of a night at the theater in New York; there is nothing quite like it. The appeal of the city reasserted itself.

Driving with the throngs of other motorists through the Holland Tunnel back to New Jersey, I marveled at the phenomenon of Manhattan, a 20-mile-long island made of granite with such a concentration of diverse, talented, and restless people. We flew back to Iowa the next day and landed to mist over green fields, quiet empty spaces, strong simple people, and the life we have chosen to live. Amidst the comfort and relief of my return home were the mixed memories of the city; exciting, interesting, disorienting, whispering in the back of my mind that life contains far more than any of us, in whatever life we lead, might suppose. We left many things undone and unseen: the Statue of Liberty, the Empire State Building, Fifth Avenue, Brooklyn Bridge, the United Nations. In case we ever need a break from all this peace and quiet and pastoral beauty, we have a place to go!

PASSING ROCKPORT

Summer 1994

Rockport always casts a spell over me. I don't know if it is the Gulf air, dense with moisture and salt from the blue-gray water, or if it is the house, built 130 years ago by my great-grandfather, or if it is the sleepy little town, seemingly immune to the developments of the late 20th Century. Whatever the reason, I know when I'm driving down 218 from San Antonio and I pass through Sinton and see that first body of water surrounded by grass and reeds with the occasional fisherman and the first gulls swooping around them looking for discarded bait that I can relax.

My great-grandfather's house is a Greek-revival Victorian "cottage." It stands on brick arches 6 feet high, enabling it to withstand the many hurricanes that sweep through the Texas Gulf Coast. The hurricane of 1919 was so devastating that the town of Rockport never recovered. It had been the most important city on the southern coast, 20,000 people strong, home of the Fulton Mathis Cattle Company and an elegant resort for traveling Texans. All of that energy shifted to Corpus Christi—which has flourished—leaving Rockport a sleepy fishing and tourist village of 5,000 people and of course my great grandfather's house.

My father bought this beautiful old house when I was 15, a gift to my mother. She was born in Rockport and played underneath the house throughout her childhood. With the house back in the family due to my father's generosity, my mother washed its exterior herself—standing on tall ladders and helped by strong teenage boys. She installed lace cur-

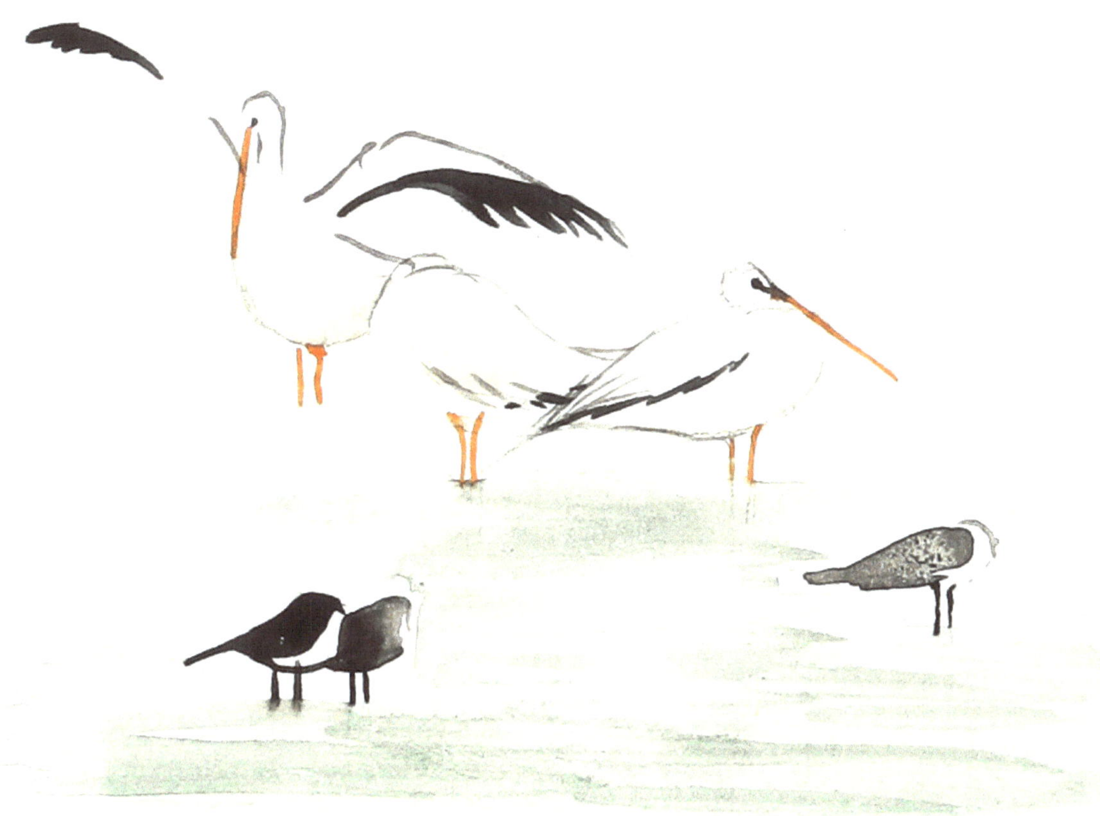

tains and brought back the antique furniture, still held by my uncle, that was originally in the house. The ceilings in the main part of the house are 15 feet high. Lying in the mahogany canopy bed and looking up at the organza folded in an intricate pattern, gathered in the center like a rose, I felt transported back to a time where my personal concerns faded and I became a witness to the distant lives of other men and women.

Rockport is bathed in the Gulf air, heavy with moisture, salt, and heat. In the summer it is like living in an herbal steam bath. We stay in my great-grandfather's house between noon and 6 PM It is too hot for almost anything else. Listening to the hum of the air conditioner in the back room, which used to be a porch but is now enclosed by stained pine beams, we congregate to work puzzles, play poker, read summer novels, discuss family history, and tell jokes with our feet propped up on the long, low maple coffee table, rocking in the chairs.

In the evening the wind comes up and blows away the heat of the day. We watch the moon come up over the water and the night fishermen come out to the long piers that protrude from the shore—one after the other, with the occasional washout where only the pillars remain. Everyone is quiet, respecting the rituals of fishing; young boys occasionally shout when their line catches in the breeze and refuses to cast out across the water. The smells of fish and salt intertwine in the moist air and blow through the people on the piers, dampening them. The water laps against the pier columns, and the lines of crab traps seem to move and sway with the rhythm.

Thoughts don't much come in Rockport. Our minds go into neutral. I used to be bored as a teenager, but as an adult I am soothed. It is the only place on earth I can walk around downtown in my bathing suit and shorts and feel relaxed. Rockport Beach is a small area surrounded on two sides by bay waters, with a ski basin and wildlife preserve on one side and the bay lapping at the shallow beach on the other. It is ideal for babies and small children because the waves are small, the shells are plentiful, the sand is soft, and the water is shallow and warm. All of my babies learned to love the water in Rockport Bay before they graduated to deep ice-cold mountain lakes and the turbulent ocean tides of Southern California. But a dip in Rockport Bay can still make me feel peaceful and remember the days when a good beach for a baby was the most important thing I could find.

The yachts of Key Allegro (the only really upscale development of the area, with large summer houses facing each other across canals) plow through the Gulf Channel, which is the route from Rockport Bay, beyond the Channel Islands, and out into the Gulf of Mexico. The waters change there, becoming choppy and a more wild blue. The offshore oil rigs and sea gulls are left behind, and the winds and the dolphins dance around the fishing boats. The shrimpers—beat-up boats with tall masts and ropes and nets intersecting across their decks—go out early in the morning and come back at varying times with their catches of large gulf shrimp. In the north they're called prawns but in Texas they're just shrimp—slimy grey creatures with crusty shells, black beady eyes, and several long hairs sticking out in front of their curved bodies.

I went down to Bea's Bait Stand at 4:30 PM to pick up some shrimp fresh off the boat for our family's dinner. Bea was a large man in height and girth. His weathered skin and the cigarette drooping from his lips displayed a disregard for medical advice that made him seem oddly liberated. He was at home in his bait stand, a dingy one-room shack piled high with coolers full of shrimp, crab, and soda. It smelled fishy and fresh at the same time as the first stirrings of a breeze came through. He spoke of his boats as if he was captain of an armada.

I took the shrimp home to my mother's kitchen, which is a combination of old and new: worn beige linoleum that salt and sand don't seem to damage, knotty pine cabinets with display niches showing old china, antique cabinets, bronze appliances, and a double sink that backs up much too frequently.

My daughters, both vegetarians, cleaned the shrimp, removing their shells and stripping away the line of black innards. They sang silly songs, giggling about their "disgusting" task, yet good-naturedly helping prepare a spread for our family that we set out on the square varnished oak table.

The grey shrimp turned a miraculous pink after 60 seconds in the large boiling pots of water. I laid them on large platters with small crystal bowls filled with spicy red sauce. Fruit salads, green salads, Vermont cheddar cheese, French bread, and huge bowls of fresh red cherries with the stems poking out completed the simple meal: something for everyone.

After dinner my brothers strung their fishing poles and took the boys out to the pier for the silent rituals of night fishing. My 80-year-old mother lay on her brass bed reading *A Suitable Boy*, and my sister-in-law and I finished the jigsaw puzzle we had all been working on over the course of our long weekend. The moon had risen over the water, which you could hear lapping the piers and shore in the distance.

I breathed the moist air, dreading the long journey planned for the next day. I remembered a ritual that friends of our family with three daughters subjected any of their serious boyfriends to. It was called "Passing Rockport," and it involved spending a weekend successfully drinking, fishing, and whittling away time at their bay-front Rockport home. If they were successful at enjoying themselves under these circumstances, they were candidates for son-in-laws. As for me, I know there is a place where nature's rhythms dominate, where a family can work a puzzle together on a summer night, and somehow, it's enough.

ART IN IOWA

Winter 1993

"I can tell you what Art is and I can tell you what is Right and what is Wrong," I boasted to my friend. It was a defensive position I found myself in after ending a discussion (read losing an argument) with my teenage daughter. I had come to my friend for consolation, finding my commonplace assumptions about life challenged in a way that only arguments between teenagers and their parents seem to accomplish. I realized that I needed to reflect further on these difficult subjects before another discussion ensued (read victory achieved). Right and Wrong in particular provided an unending assortment of possible understandings and proofs. I decided to begin with Art and work my way back to Right and Wrong.

Art is like Love. It is hard to give a comprehensive definition of it, but you know it when you experience it. You also know it when it's missing. We moved to a small town in the Midwest 11 years ago. We had moved from California, not usually associated with high culture but high enough to give us the American Ballet Theatre at the Dorothy Chandler Pavilion, *The Seven Samurai* at the Toho Rio Theater, and Miles Davis live at the Greek Theatre. We came to this small Midwest town and realized that Art was not ornamental in our lives, not something to do on the weekends, but something vital that we couldn't live without. So we set about finding art in Iowa. Along with some inspired friends, we started a cultural society, importing artists to our town. We sought out events

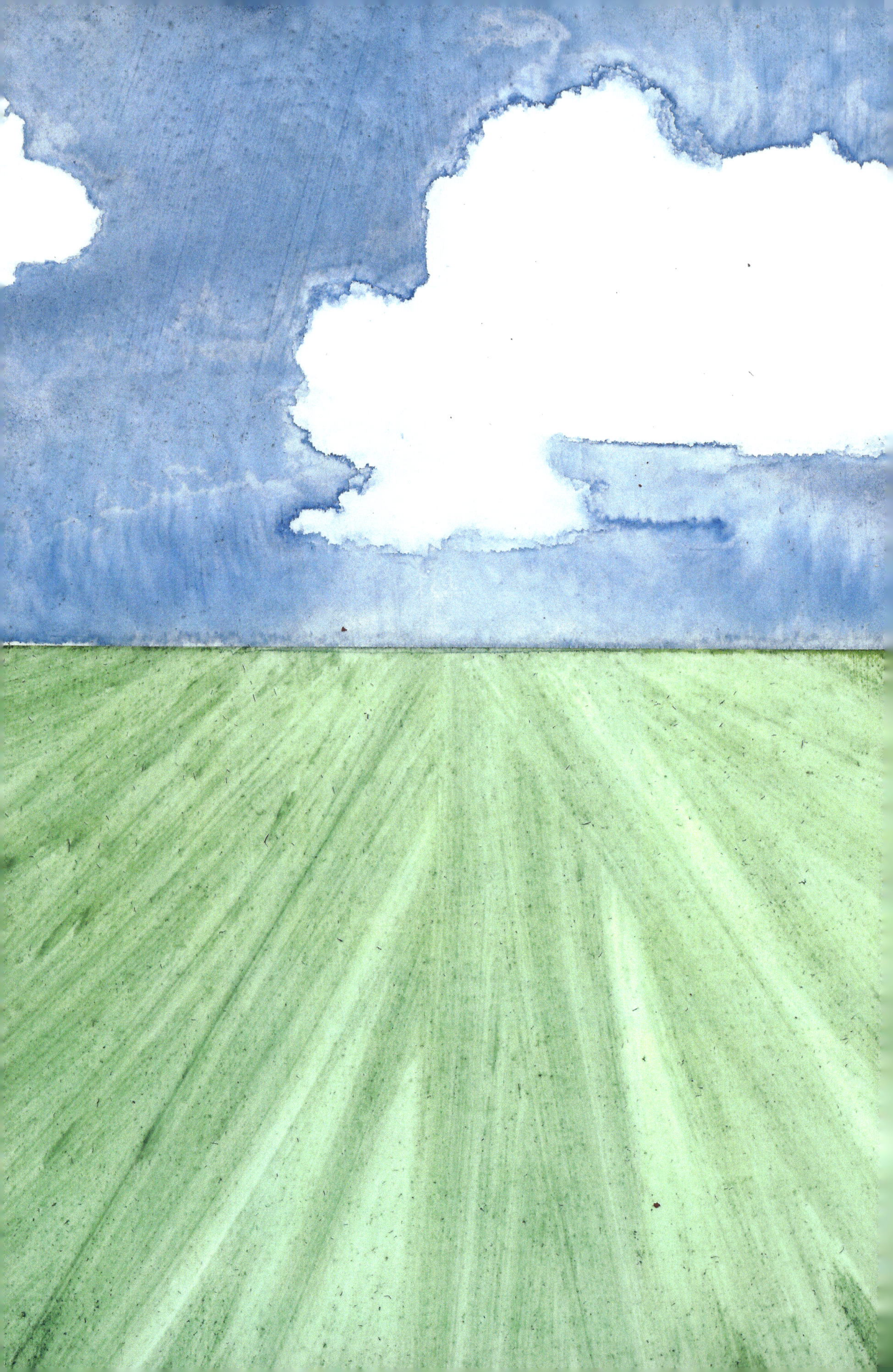

in nearby areas: Hancher Auditorium in Iowa City, musical theater in Chicago, and symphony in St. Louis. Stimulated by the cold, empty Midwestern winters, we also discovered Art within ourselves. These lookings, missings, and findings led me to some personal understandings about what Art (meaning all of the Arts) is, and I tremulously share them with you now.

Art is a knitting together of the deeper inner values of life with the surface, obvious levels. It begins with the personal and penetrates to the universal. This definition implies an intrinsic value to life—that deeper levels of reality and experience render more and more of its essential content. This is not a popular approach in the 20th Century, which has been dominated by the existential position that life is defined by meaningful action. The notion that life itself is infinite potential, resting in silence within each part of itself, makes Art all the more essential, for it has the power to create connections to this vital inner reality.

Art is by its nature uplifting. It expands life in the sense that it gives a bigger context to ordinary (or extraordinary) events and a deeper value to sensual, emotional, and intellectual experience. This is not to say that Art is by nature pleasant. Entertainment is pleasant or enjoyable, attractive, or distracting. But Art must be described as uplifting because it unites us with a bigger wholeness—transforming, moving, expanding, stimulating, and enlightening us in the process.

I could not teach anyone how to become an Artist; I am still cultivating those tendencies for myself. But I have discovered some qualities which, when developed, help with the apprehension and appreciation of Art. Silence, the most basic, allows the unbounded potential of life to create a wholeness from which understanding inevitably emerges. I remember the first time I saw the Cathedral at Chartres, France. Its Gothic spires rise to the heavens and form arches that cradle the most beautiful stained glass windows in the world. It rests on a hill in the old town, crowded by streets and buildings but standing in the dignity of its own beauty despite the incongruity of the 20th Century encroaching upon its natural boundaries. Inside one finds silence, an emptiness bound by the shapes of the cathedral and relieved by the sunlight shining through the colored windows onto the stone floors. As the silence engulfed me, I thought of the architects and church leaders who conceived this building, the many craftsmen who over centuries built it—the sacrifices they must have made—and the transforming power of its vision as it evolved. It is a work of Art for the ages.

Art can sometimes be found in unexpected places if one cultivates a state of receptivity. The first time I went snorkeling on the island of Maui, Hawaii, I had an experience that awakened new possibilities for me. As I dove into the water and began my inspection of the sea below the surface, I was engulfed by schools of tropical fish. There were translucent cobalt blue fish, golden knife-edged fish with black markings circling their eyes, fluorescent orange fish with tissue-thin tails trailing after their bodies—a seemingly endless variety. Gazing at the hundreds, maybe thousands of fish that surrounded me, brushing against my legs as they hurried by, caused me great wonder. Why were they here? What was the purpose of having something so extraordinarily beautiful, varied, and delicate beneath the surface of the dark, deep ocean, unseen except by the occasional swimmer? This must be one of the Creator's masterpieces. It transformed me by showing me that beauty exists independent of meaning, for its own sake, and it can be found in private places, relying only on the gaze of the seeker and her receptivity—her ability to recognize the infinite potential residing beneath her own gaze.

Intelligence, a third quality, develops the ability to consider the principles of proportion, balance, contrast, harmony, and integrity within any individual work of Art. The enlivenment of intelligence integrated with the expansion of feeling is the core of any artistic experience. Recently I was in Chicago with my family and had the opportunity to hear the Chicago Symphony live in Orchestra Hall. The program was all Russian, with

Russian composers, conductor, and pianist. One of the pieces they played was a Prokofiev concerto. The conductor, a tall slim man with a shock of dark hair, bounded onto the stage with the most alert expression I have ever seen on a performer. The pianist followed—a short, stocky, bald man who conveyed dignity by the intensity of purpose reflected in his face. When the music began I understood their challenge. It was a big piece, dense with music, full of immense contrasts, from mournful melodies to bombastic dissonant passages and from quiet interludes to thundering climaxes. The musicians moved quickly through the complex music, mastering it with their intense concentration, superb musicality, and superior skills. They along with the audience were caught in the momentum of the music and the incredible blend of intelligence and feeling communicated. The string players' elbows moved in quick synchrony, and the percussive sounds were augmented by the bold gestures of the players. At the end of the piece the audience gave rapturous applause while the symphony musicians themselves applauded the conductor and soloist. We were transformed: feeling fully alert, settled, yet far more alive than when we had entered the hall. As we emerged we noticed the faces of our fellow audience members filled with intelligence and refinement. The music had done its job.

Self-expression is not Art, though it may become a stepping stone in that process. It only becomes Art when the "self" expressed becomes big enough to encompass universal values and create a connectedness between ourselves and others. We make "a community of sorts" with our audience, thereby laying a foundation for communication and commitment. As Wendell Berry says, Art defines "our commonwealth" as well as enlarging it. It helps us to express individuality as well as to create community, and when it is successful it ties the two together in a bond of reciprocal support and ongoing evolution.

Many interesting questions remain about Art, bearing further reflection and discussion (read our daughter is turning 21 soon). For example, can real Art be found in popular culture? Is there a state where Art ceases to be necessary, where life itself becomes Art? How do we identify the standards which govern our intuitive judgments about Art? How much authorship is actually involved in creating a work of Art?

Frankly, I'm glad there is so much to think about with regard to Art. I look over my shoulder and I see Right and Wrong hovering there, demanding definition to support all the "guidelines" I have foisted upon my children. I see mountains of personal responsibility, moral dilemmas at every turn, the slippery road of "situational" ethics, and truly modern malaises like genetic engineering and cloning. I am not giving up on Right and Wrong, but on balance I'd have to say that Art is more comfortable to think about. Like Love, when we come to the end of the idea of it, we simply experience it, and we find that it is its own justification.

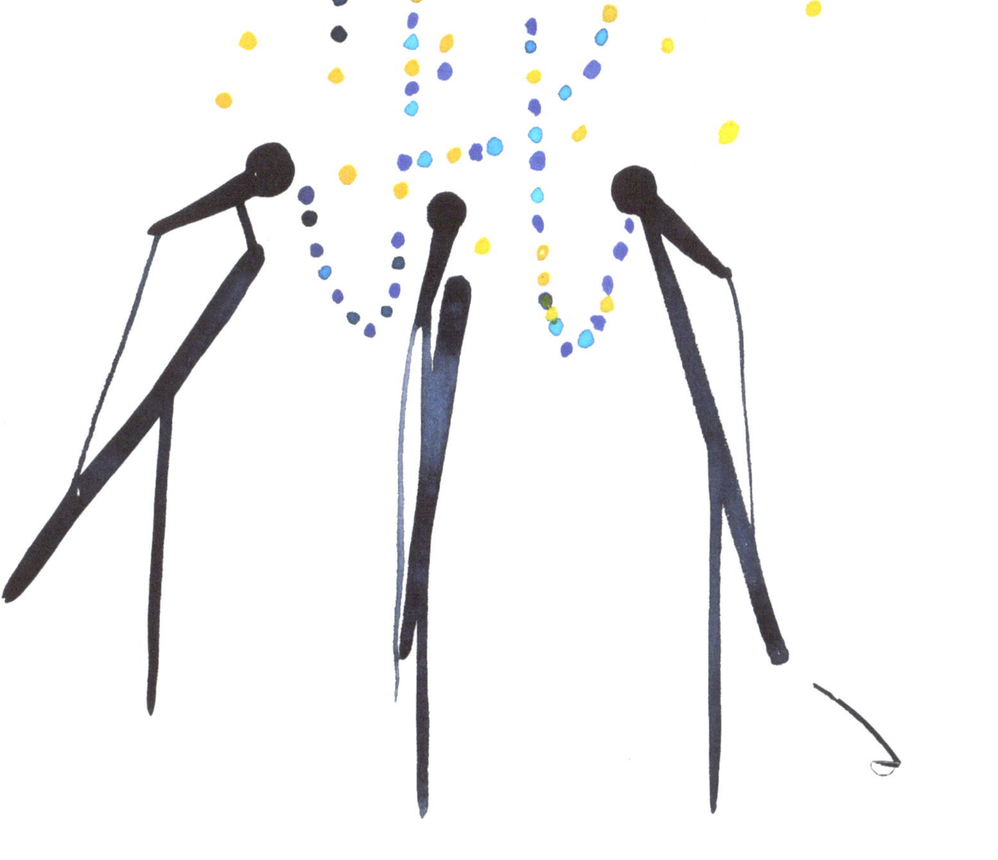

REUNION II

Winter 2002

"Turn on your light," my husband screamed. "Let it shine on me." He wasn't shrieking for attention after nearly 35 years of marriage. He was singing—singing at a reunion—a reunion of the rock band he had started 38 years ago. It predated me. But I did jump on board, and not as a groupie, as I have so often been accused, but as a girlfriend. There was a difference. I was his "old lady" who became his young wife on his 21st birthday over 35 years ago. The reunion was necessary because the band broke up shortly after our wedding. We hadn't seen some of the people since, even though they played at our wedding, which was held in my brother's backyard in Marin County—me in a white organza mini-dress and him in a Nehru jacket and beads.

Despite the alternative beginning, we have had a remarkably traditional marriage, with three fantastic children and lots of connections to our extended families. Riding back in time to see our hippie friends, who of course aren't hippies anymore, but who remember us as wild, uninhibited trailblazers, had an allure for us.

Reunions by their nature are a study in the role that memory plays in identity. We carry each phase of our life, each incarnation of ourselves—our childhood, adolescence, college years, parenthood, and middle age—as pieces in our overall mosaic of self. To isolate one, especially one so far distant, sets up a dynamic of recognition, rebuttal, and redefinition.

For us it was an affectionate look back, beginning with an email from Gail, the new wife of the rhythm guitar player. The legend of *The Loading Zone* had sparked her imagination. She wanted to rent the Fillmore West and recreate the many nights *The Zone* played there, opening for the great bands of the '60s: The Who, Cream, Janis Joplin, Lightnin' Hopkins, Chuck Berry, The Grateful Dead, and Jefferson Airplane. But that proved too much in all ways. Gail said she would find a place on the peninsula near their home in Los Gatos, and could we come January 11th?

As it happened, Paul had work in California just after that, so we decided to go. Linda, the other lead singer, would be there, as well as the bass player, drummers, soundman, roadies, wives, and fans. The lead guitar player and horn players wouldn't be there. As one of the band members said, "We should do this while we are all still ambulatory."

Of the nine members of *The Loading Zone* who recorded on RCA in 1968, three are still in the music business: my music producer husband Paul; Linda, a performing legend and musicologist in the bay area; and Todd, a horn player working in New York. Of the previous band members, two are computer programmers and one is a newscaster. One died of a drug overdose several years after the band broke up, and the only one to follow the hippie dream makes thumb pianos in the Dominican Republic and is known as Papi Loco.

We spent days combing through old pictures, made a new poster in the old style (with the help of our artist daughter), and took our new poster to Kinko's to make copies for the band members. It read *The Loading Zone*, One Night Only at Rolling Manor (the retirement community rec room Gail had decided on), formerly known as "The Lucky 13 Club" (a former Zone haunt), Seniors Welcome. We don't know if they got the jokes because the lights were low, the wine was flowing, and we were all so amazed to see each other.

Paul and I had spent a long time planning our "outfits." Paul broke a major fashion rule in our household and went with an all-jean ensemble. My brother's wife, who lives two doors away, has a set of bandanas she uses for Southwestern entertaining, and she gave Paul a choice of bright pink, chartreuse green, brown, or mauve. He then recreated the '60s with a mauve bandana, worn across his forehead. He also visited a "head shop" on the Old Austin Highway, swearing that it was the abode of Satan and he would never return; nevertheless he found some important accessories—buttons of various sizes, colors, and designs (Does anyone remember buttons?).

His choices were good, with many instructive messages: *Who Needs Hair, Anyway; I Need To Refinance My Karmic Debt; Another Cynical Ex-Hippie Now Working For The Establishment; Question Reality!; Help, I Think I'm A Rock Star; Curious George; I Am Doing My Part, Are You?* These he placed strategically on his jeans jacket, along with an Elvis two-way and a Gene Autry button he already owned, plus his father's World War II medal. Add some coral and turquoise beads he gave me a few years ago, and he was set. He wore his Christmas present, Lucchese cowboy boots, because we now live in Texas, to finish things off. He looked great!

My apparel was a harder project. I used to make all my own clothes, and they were usually micro-mini numbers. I have pretty much permanently switched to tunics and pants these days, for obvious reasons. I ended up with a velvet tunic, black jeans, a beret with a Yin/Yang button and the Frank Zappa message *Without Deviation from the Norm, Progress Is Not Possible*, and a long leather jacket. I looked like a plump, well-to-do church lady with a beret. Oh well.

We drove to the event with old friends from Berkeley who had been fans of *The Zone*. They were billed as "videographers." Their BMW's navigating system led us off the freeway and through the outskirts of Los Gatos to Rolling Manor, a retirement community. We were scared as we approached the clubhouse; this was the kind of place we avoid, thinking we'll never want it or need it.

The party room had a low ceiling with about 10 round tables, each set for eight. There was a lava lamp, low lighting, and album covers from the '60s were mounted on the walls. We added our poster to the display and ordered some wine to fortify us. Pieter, the roadie, looked very authentic in a chambray shirt, vest, and wig, with bandana. Bob, the bass player, had an orange tie-dyed t-shirt, a long black-haired wig, and his reluctant 13-year-old in tow. The soundman looked the same as he did in the '60s—white undershirt, Brooks Brothers shirt, and a modified Afro.

Linda, the female lead singer, looked fantastic. When she came to audition for *The Zone* in 1967, she worked for the post office, weighed 300 pounds, and had straight processed hair, plus a voice that brought life to the R&B sound of the band. Since then she has shed the weight, the hairdo, and the inexperience and developed into a beautiful, powerful soul singer and musicologist who tours the world as Linda Tillery and the Cultural Heritage Choir.

As the night progressed, Paul performed a few songs, "Knock On Wood" and "Turn On Your Love Light," and Linda also performed with the band hired for the occasion, *East Bay Mud*, a nine-member R&B cover band with three horns and two lead singers. Paul then announced an experiment. *The Zone* would play together for the first time in 35 years. Linda wisely declined.

Bob, the bass player, gamely started his descending arpeggios to begin "2120 South Michigan Avenue" with drummer number 1, Ted, who had had a liver transplant and cardiac arrest within the past 3 years. It was tentative R&B, not at all like the hard-driving, raw, exciting sound of earlier years, but all in all, not embarrassing. Then drummer number 2, George, joined in and the singing began. What can I say? The birthday boy, Steve, began "Land of 1,000 Dances" very softly. He is a fresh-faced man who became a software engineer at Cisco Systems and is now retired. By the end of the song, we could hear him!

At evening's end, we said goodbye. Paul and Linda promised to work together. I wished friends good health, promised Nancy to call about teaching English as a Second Language (ESL), thanked Steve and his wife, relayed effusive goodbyes to the unhappy teen, and gave hugs to various people.

Some people never look back, preferring to focus on the future; others live in the past, with vivid memories and recollections permeating their present days. We prefer to live in an ever-expanding upward spiral, revisiting former experiences, places, and friends with deeper understandings and more generous interpretations. We are living in Texas again, where I was born and raised and where we lived when our two daughters were born. It has been deeply satisfying to be home and to see how things have changed and grown. If our spiral theory holds true, we should be in for big amounts of travel, meditation, and childcare. That's fine with me. What I'm not sure about is my 40th high school reunion next year. Wish me luck on that one!

LAND OF ENCHANTMENT

Spring 2006

I never realized there was a problem between New Mexico and Texas until I visited Roswell, New Mexico and had a conversation with Steve, the director of the artist residency program that my daughter Joey was participating in. "Texans think everything they have is so great—their trees are the best, their people are the best, their cities are the best. We don't think they're so great. There are hundreds of Texans here; as a matter of fact they call this 'Little Texas,' but they don't know we don't like them." I tried to be diplomatic. As a Texan, born and raised, I understood what he was talking about. "We're just enthusiastic," I said. "We also think we have the best neighbors!" "Yeah, yeah, I know. But Texas gave New Mexico the raw end of the stick when we became a state in 1912. They redrew the borders. Texas ends where the good land ends and New Mexico starts where the badlands start."

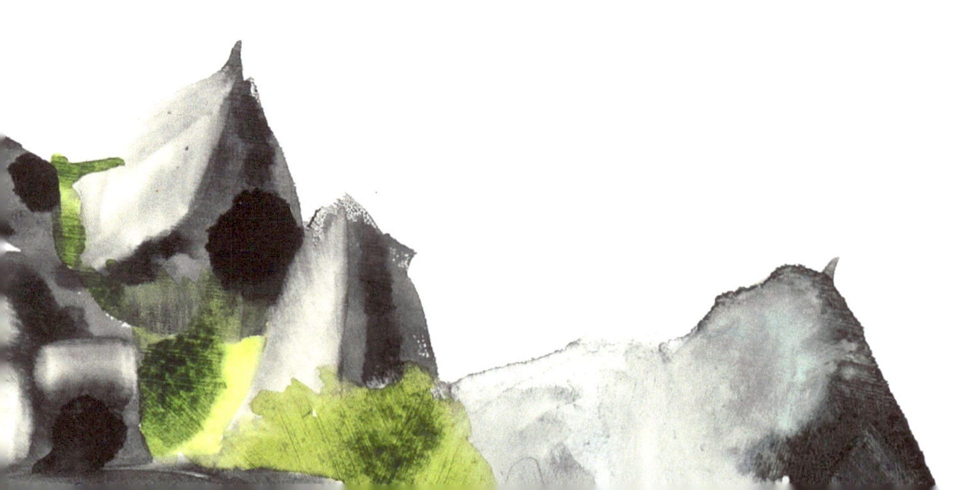

I don't agree. I drove through West Texas last month along Interstate 10 to Fort Stockton and cut up 285 to Roswell to visit Joey on her 29th birthday. I'll admit the West Texas country around Junction and Sonora is gorgeous, and the windmills on the mountainous horizon as the hill country flattens out are dramatic and surreal—like giant art installations. Still I like the New Mexico state motto, "Land of Enchantment." It is bad, it is dry, but wow, it is exciting!

Driving toward southeastern New Mexico, one passes through Pecos, Texas. That's the home of Pecos Bill, the cartoon character who lassoed the dirt funnels that really do sweep through West Texas and New Mexico. You see them in the distance as you drive the empty road between Pecos and Roswell. You also see tumbleweeds everywhere. I was reminded of the Pecos Bill cartoon in which the lady bounces on her bustle at the top of the wind funnel, and of the old country tune, *Tumbling Tumbleweeds*.

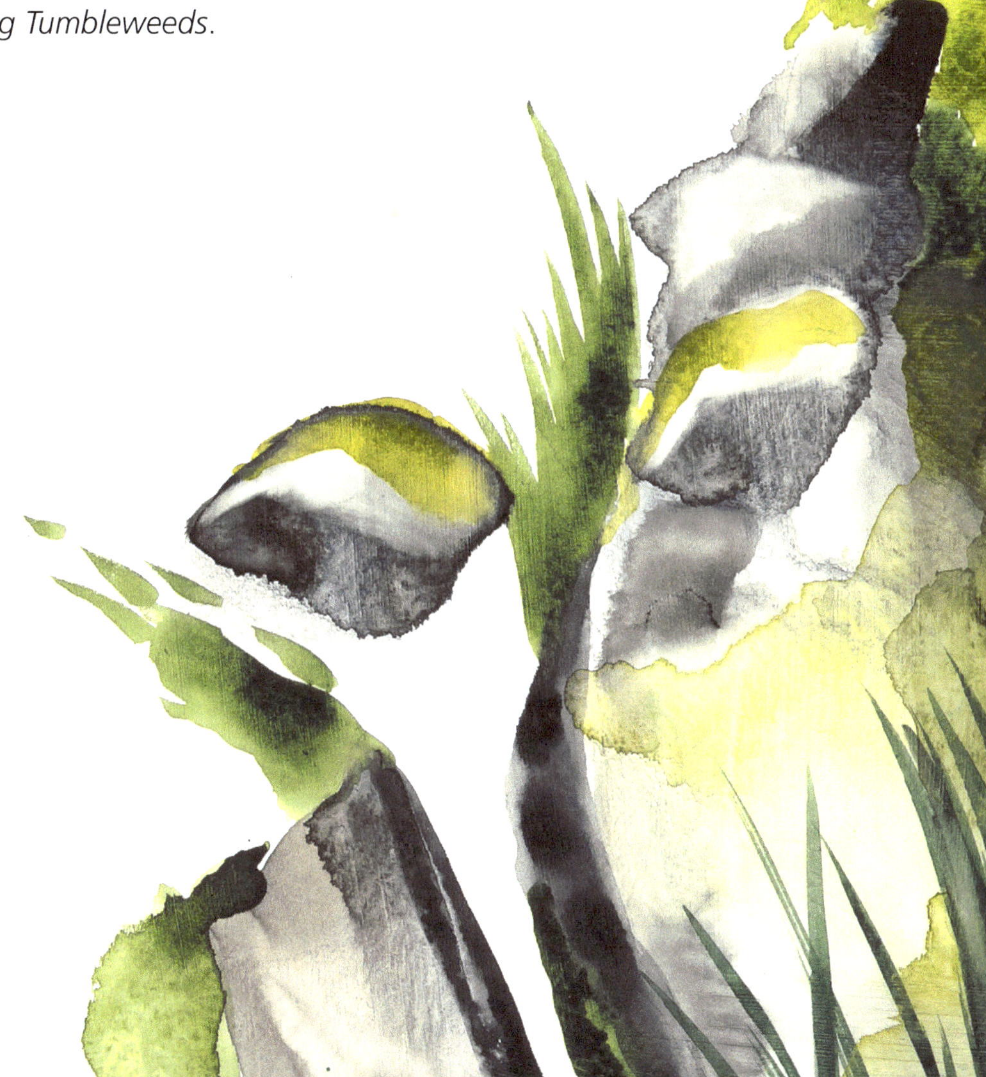

The first indication that New Mexico is seriously enchanted is found in Carlsbad, a seemingly normal small city. On its outskirts is Carlsbad Caverns, a National Park. A few years ago we were driving through on the way to visit our friends in Wyoming via Roswell to see the UFO museum (we think my husband Paul may be an alien because he was born 7.7.1947, when the UFOs landed in Roswell). Although it was late in the afternoon when we reached Carlsbad, we took a chance and made the turn into the Park, where it suddenly became beautiful—gorges filled with Joshua trees and every variety of cactus there is. We passed the bat cave where thousands of bats fly out every evening, entered the large Park building with displays and gift shops, and caught the last oversized elevator to go 100 feet below the earth's surface to see one of the largest caves in North America. The elevator opened to "rooms" with 30-foot-high domed "ceilings" and stalactite/stalagmite formations so odd and interesting that only in dreams could you have seen anything like them. At one point they turned the already-dimmed lights completely off. If you're a little claustrophobic like I am, this is going to present a challenge to you. I began the pant/blow operation I had learned in my Lamaze classes 30 years earlier while Paul communed with the darkness. It was darker than anything we had ever seen, and if you've never been significantly below the earth's surface, you won't have experienced darkness. The earth's surface rests on this core of dark empty silence, and it makes you wonder about the relationships of silence and activity, darkness and light, eternity and time. I am not sure how all those things are related, but that's what came to our minds.

When we emerged, dusk was falling on the high desert landscape, and we were grateful to be on the beautiful surface of New Mexico once again. As we drove towards Roswell, we saw signs for White Sands National Park, an intriguing name for sure and one that caused me to remember a photo of my mother from the '40s. She and my father and their then only child (my oldest brother) visited White Sands. In the photo documenting the event, she was wearing a long red flowing dress and sandals, sitting on a sand dune with a pensive expression on her beautiful face and nothing but white sand and a cobalt blue sky behind her. It was one of those photos that guides a child's imagination and creates her impression of her mother's life outside the bounds of their relationship. Mother was enchanted with New Mexico, and I was enchanted with mother. This long arm of mystery and beauty must be what draws me back to New Mexico over and over again.

The most amazing drive I remember was outside of Taos, heading toward the Colorado border. There the Rio Grande River cuts a deep gorge in an otherwise completely flat landscape that, in the far distance, is surrounded on all sides by a circle of towering mountains. We could not help but think that we were entering a gathering place for Native American gods. Driving across the mesa, crossing the Rio Grande, and heading to the mountains felt laden with importance. A further reward was seeing herds of wild horses in the beautiful mountains of northwestern New Mexico.

One year I made the trip alone, my first journey as a solo road warrior. It took about 8 hours from our home in the Texas Hill Country—out Highway 290, connecting to Interstate 10 just northwest of Kerrville, and finally heading due north on 285—to Roswell, which is a clean, friendly town with three interesting museums, a military school, and (apparently) a lot of expat Texans. If you continue up 285, as Joey and I did the day after I arrived, you'll come to the beautiful enchanted city of Santa Fe. It is the oldest continuous seat of government in our country, now capital of the state of New Mexico, and home to many outstanding museums. Joey and I spent her birthday visiting six of those museums: Site Santa Fe (contemporary art), the Georgia O'Keeffe Museum, Santa Fe Fine Art Museum, The Governor's Palace, The Folk Art Museum, and The Native American Museum. There are also many art galleries and fancy shops as well as street vendors selling Native American-made jewelry, baskets,

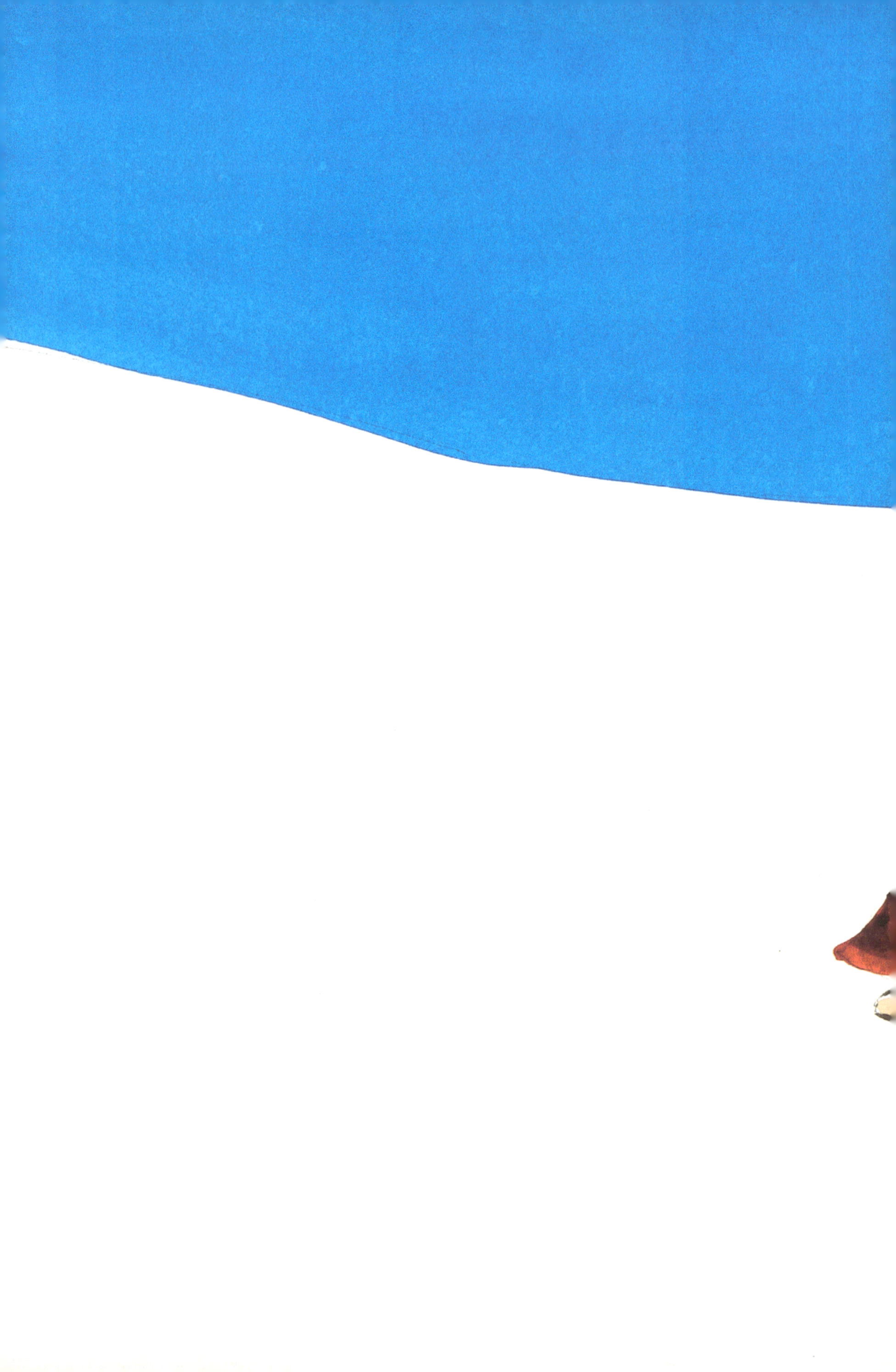

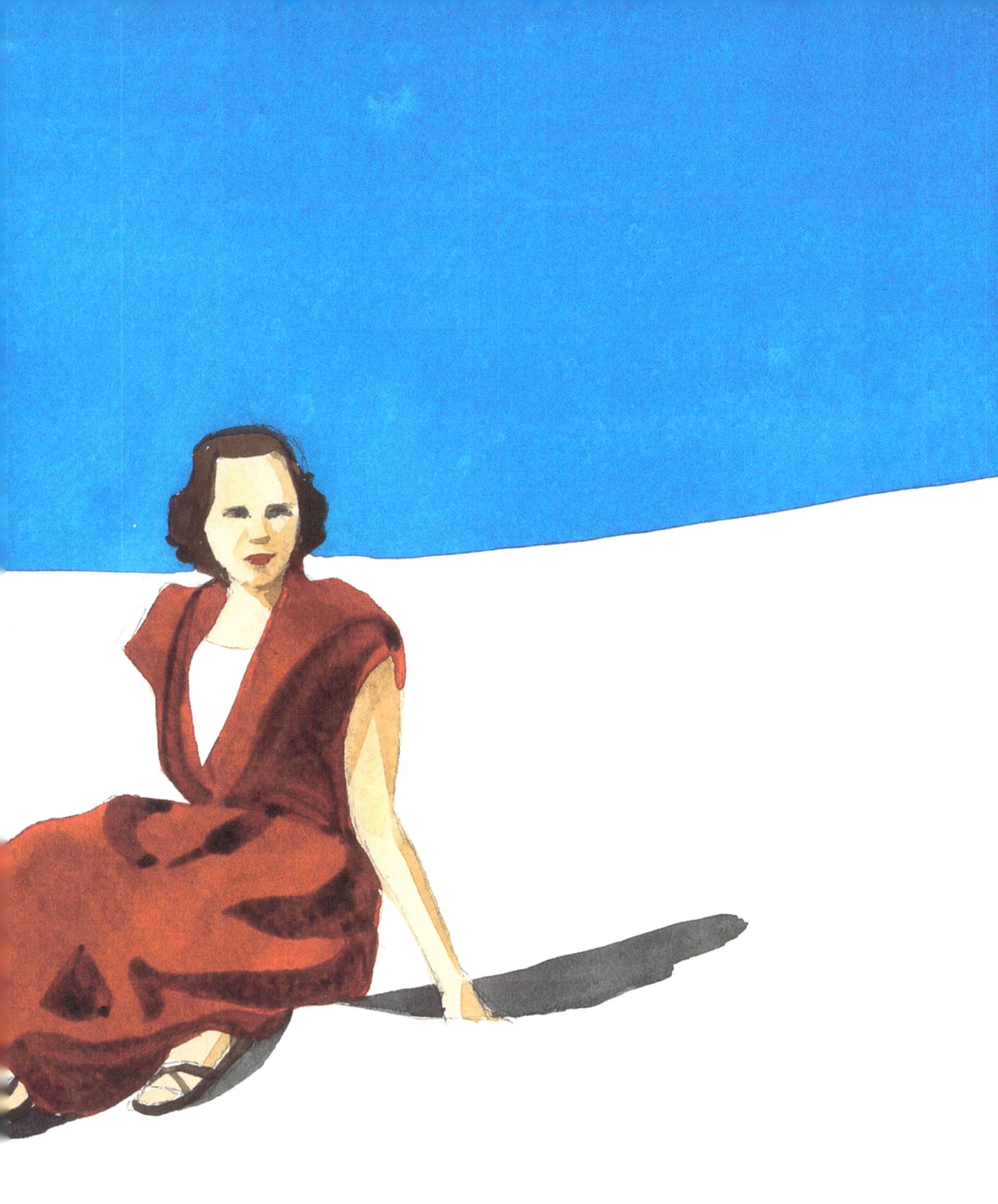

and textiles.

Santa Fe hosts many festivals throughout the year, during which the square turns into open markets and exhibits for contemporary art and traditional Indian crafts. Characters may be seen everywhere. On our latest trip we ran into a man with a dog on a leash and a cat on his back licking a little white mouse—all live animals. Women really dress in the Southwest style there, with lots of turquoise jewelry, drapey clothes, big belts, and long hair with giant earrings.

The Santa Fe Opera is also an exciting event. Wind, rain, and moonlight frame the amazing world-famous opera house, open to the elements on the sides, with overhanging roofs to protect the audience and performers from the weather. The musicians and singers are world-class, and the programs vary from traditional favorites to world premieres. We saw an American premiere of the opera Tea, Mirror of the Soul by Tan Dun, the composer of the score for the film Crouching Tiger, Hidden Dragon. It was extraordinary, very moving, creative, and innovative, with all kinds of unusual percussive elements, from paper being torn to cups being pounded on water.

The food in Santa Fe is especially good, whether New Mexican (very different from Mexican or Tex/Mex, as natives are quick to point out) or Continental. Joey and I ate at a place specializing in New Mexican cuisine called The Shed, a very popular spot (we waited 45 minutes for a table) with a courtyard and a waiting area with a traditional adobe fireplace. We sat on a bench next to the fire, watched the many people come and go, and decided that white athletic shoes look bad with every possible outfit, on men or women, old or young.

The next morning took us to the mineral baths of Ojo Caliente, an hour north of Santa Fe. Mud baths and waters with sulfur and arsenic are the specialties. For me the best feature was the deep blue sky that framed the spa, surpassing the West Texas skies that I have loved all my life. It even surpassed the Sierra skies! It is why Georgia O'Keeffe,

America's most famous female artist of the 20th Century, moved to New Mexico. She painted those skies over and again, along with many other artists, known and unknown.

Thoroughly relaxed, we headed back to Roswell for a dinner at Pasta Café, Roswell's newest restaurant and not half bad at that. We watched two movies at Joey's house in the compound and slept soundly in the quiet New Mexican night filled with fresh, sweet, dry air. I was sad to leave my daughter and New Mexico. The Texas State Troopers greeted me with a speeding ticket and a smile, and I completed my first interstate solo journey unharmed.

My next trip to Roswell was with my husband and my son Neil. We were going to attend Joey's opening at the Roswell Museum of Art, the culmination of her yearlong residency. The weekend was dramatic and filled with contrasts. Her opening was a great success. She had spent the year in a very dedicated way: making art that was both personal and universal, profound and appealing. She filled the museum's exhibition space, and everyone from her program, as well as art lovers from the area, attended. At the same time, a terrible accident occurred that involved Molly, a friend of Joey's in the same program. Molly was with a young man from Roswell when he fell through a ceiling and broke his back, becoming paralyzed. Molly couldn't come to any of the events, and we were constantly worried about her friend and the accident's implications for both of their lives.

Joey had come to know some of the area's resident artists, and we visited their workspaces. William Goodman, a small Englishman who makes giant steel sculpture, invited us to his compound, an old motel with several houses and an old storefront. His steel pieces were interspersed with the buildings, all set in a dusty landscape that created an intriguing if forlorn atmosphere. His studio, as tall as it was wide and long, housed heavy tools for forging his creations. His home was modest, even austere, with a small cot-like bed. Kitchen appliances dated from the '40s, and a shortwave radio with old leather earphones was his only visible connection to the outside world.

Further up the road we visited the studio of Louis Jimenez, the well-known artist who makes giant fiberglass sculptures for public art. His compound was an old apple processing plant, apparently from the days when apple orchards were abundant in this area of New Mexico.

Louis met us there and instantly bonded with Paul. He showed us the small models of his sculpture, the huge fiberglass molds, and several pieces that were either finished or in process. The most impressive was a giant blue Mustang horse, meant for the entry to the Denver International Airport. He said he had been working on the piece for 20 years, modifying it all through the process, and that it would probably kill him. We all laughed, admiring his very impressive work. Louis was a tall handsome man with one glass eye, a result of a work-related accident. Fiberglass is a dangerous medium to work in, and given the scale of his work, I couldn't help but think that his was a dangerous enterprise. Two weeks later, when we were safely back in Texas, we heard that there had been an accident. The 20-foot high horse had fallen on Louis as he was painting it. It cut an artery in Louis's neck, and he bled to death on the way to the hospital. Another terrible tragedy; the memory of that day is still vivid in my mind. New Mexico makes its mark in both bad and good ways.

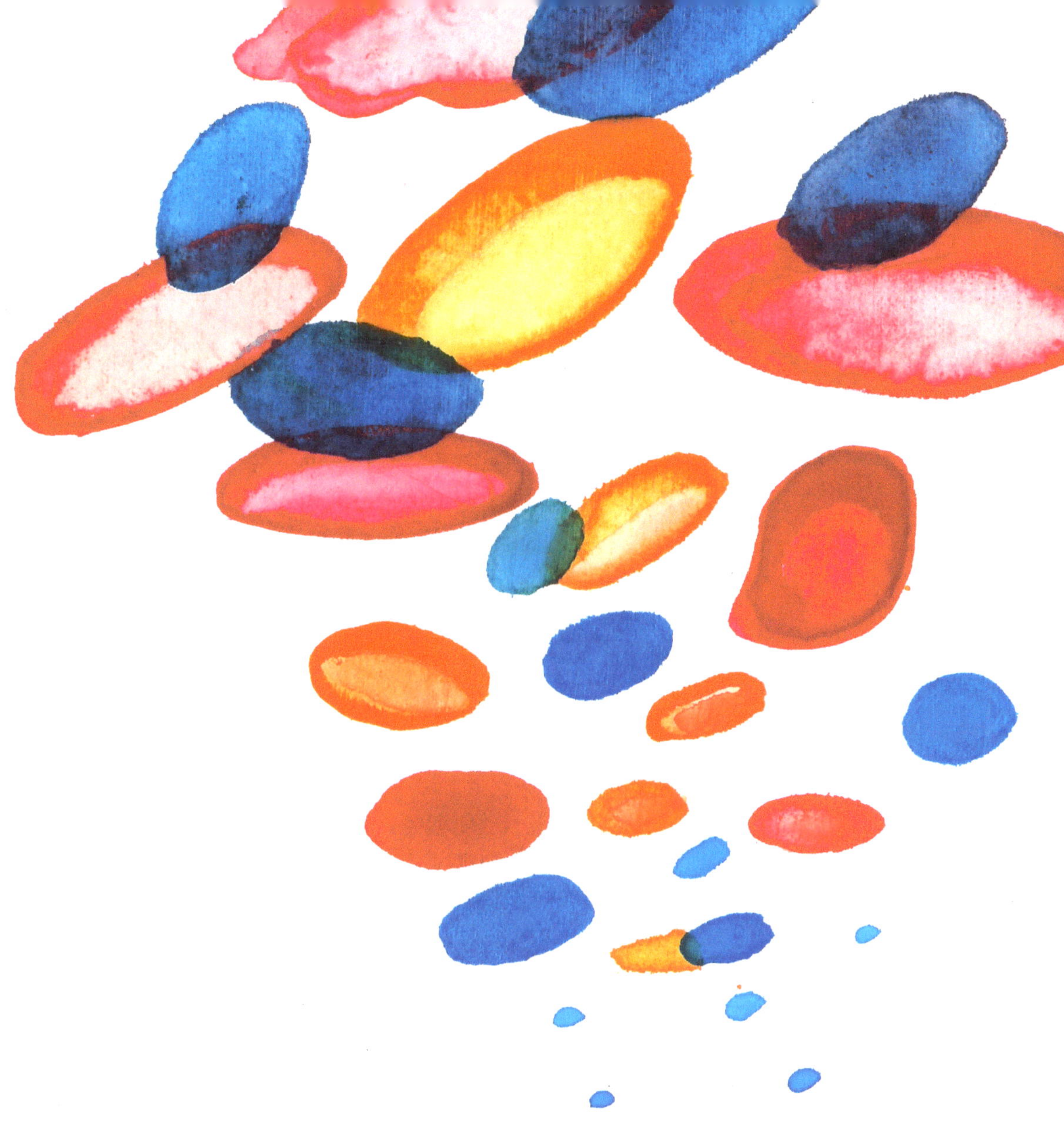

LOVE IN LAS VEGAS

Summer 2007

Las Vegas, full of couples and people who are looking to "hook up," is not a good place to go when you want to be alone. The city's tag line, which has been adopted in their advertising—Las Vegas, What Happens Here, Stays Here—gives permission to all of these people to have a time of it: maybe romantic for the couples, adventurous for the singles. All of the young women dress up in low-cut dresses, jewelry, and high heels.

Forty-eight million people visit Las Vegas every year. When we were there last August, and the temperature was over 109 degrees, we were joined on the streets and in the casinos by people from all over the world. We saw Spaniards, Colombians, Koreans, Chinese, Japanese, English, Germans, Austrians, and Italians, as well as Muslim women with headscarves, many families, and overweight couples in mirror-image shorts and baggy t-shirts.

We stayed at the Bellagio, the giant luxury hotel modeled on an Italian villa, on a summer special that was discounted for the off-season (although I don't really think Vegas has an off-season). The action starts at night, revving up as the evening unfolds. The Bellagio has lagoons in front of the main building that feature dancing fountains (think Disney's Epcot Center) choreographed to music pumped into the street through a vast speaker system. There were classical pieces, Frank Sinatra, and my favorite—Elvis singing *Viva Las Vegas*. At midnight, while we were staggering off to bed, more people could be found in the lobby and casino (same thing) than at noon; throngs of people were everywhere. Las Vegas is a fantasyland and what the rest of the world thinks America is—artificial, luxurious, loud, and with the best shopping and eating anywhere.

Two days is our maximum. We stay there en route from California to Texas; it's a pretty good stopover and was especially appealing this summer because we wanted to see a show. Famous for its entertainment, Las Vegas was started by entertainers (remember the Rat Pack?) and features a wide variety of singers, dancers, magicians, and circus performers. We were going to see *Love*, a special production of the Cirque du Soleil, the innovative Canadian circus, choreographed to the music of the Beatles. We grew up listening to Beatles music, and my musician husband regards it very highly indeed. A remix of original Beatles music by George Martin and his son was used for this production, and the sound system alone was worth the 100-dollar-plus tickets. I have never heard sound like that, from both inside and out of the theater-in-the-round. The performers swept across the stage with high wires attached to their bodies, accented by the pulsing music:

Because the world is round, it turns me on,
Because the sky is blue, it blows my mind,
Love is all,
Love is new...

The '60s lingo rang a bell for the many baby boomers in the crowd. It had poignancy to it, all that singing about peace and love. It made me feel like I did on September 11—that our generation had failed to change anything. Perhaps that's when we grew up and acknowledged the dark side of human nature. But on that night in Las Vegas we felt peace and love and possibility and even our own youth visualized through incredible lights and fog and acrobats and costumes and the sounds we associated with the New World Order that of course never happened. Instead we have Las Vegas: crass, bright, bulging with people from all over the world who have come to taste the American dream.

On our way home we stopped in southern Colorado to visit friends who also happen to be the parents of our son-in-law. They live in an idyllic cabin outside Durango and generously host their friends with a variety of adventurous treks through the beautiful mountains that surround their home.

Fifteen thousand years ago there were glaciers in Colorado. Some were a half-mile thick, and they cut through the San Juan Mountains, gouging out narrow valleys and leaving sheer cliffs that expose the red rock, filled with iron ore. We drove from one of these valleys to another over the Ophir Pass, from Durango to Telluride. The road diverged from scenic Highway 550 just past Silverton, the old mining town. We turned left onto a dirt road, which proceeded to climb 2,000 feet to the top of the pass along the sides of mountains, through spruce and fir forest and overlooking ribbons of rivers at the bottom of the gorge. The scene was definitely alpine and reminded us of the Alps in Switzerland. The wildflowers were extraordinary: wild columbine, vivid blue wild delphinium, paintbrushes of every hue of red, and wild daisies of every variety. We drove along the side of the canyon, ascending to the top and pulling over to allow a 4-wheel-drive vehicle to pass excruciatingly close to our car and to the edge of the dirt road. I could imagine falling over the edge, tumbling and sliding down the rock shale ledge to land upside down at the far bottom, smashed to smithereens like the truck we saw back on Highway 550 whose driver lost his brakes going down one of the very steep inclines on that blacktop road. This road was dirt, with rocks and boulders strewn across it, and we were in our friends' Dodge Durango, motoring in a jerky up-and-down motion through the pass.

At one point we pulled over. Paul and David, having brought their kazoos, launched into an impromptu rendition of *The Sound of Music*. We drove through the all-shale side of a mountain, passing Tinglefoot Point, so named because our daughter (David's daughter-in-law), who'd taken this same trip, had refused to exit the SUV because she claimed to have "tinglefoot." That was just before she married their son on a mountaintop just north of Durango. I think that Love in Colorado has deeper roots and brighter prospects than Love in Las Vegas.

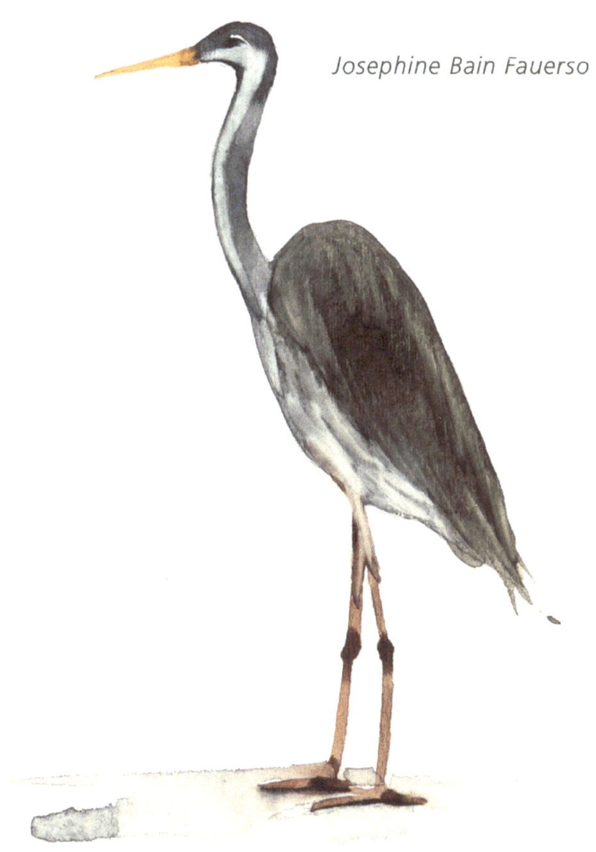

WHY I LIVE IN TEXAS

Spring 2008

Driving through these no-account towns, sometimes I wonder why I live in Texas. It's true; I grew up here and have many fond memories of my childhood in San Antonio, West Texas, the Hill Country, and the Coast. But some of these towns are really depressing and rundown, with a shabby bar and a filling station that occupies a broke-down automotive building. Just when I think I'm crazy, the land changes, opens up, and I am reminded of why I live here. The sky is big, deep blue with light swirling clouds. The wind blows sweet. I love the experience of driving through flat, scrubby country and seeing the land open to the sky and the earth rise up in hills and mountains to meet it. West Texas is rough, but it's beautiful. There are even cowboy poets out here. When you get high in the mountains, the air cools and the Ponderosa Pine and Douglas Fir mix with the native cactus and yucca bushes to give off a delicious scent.

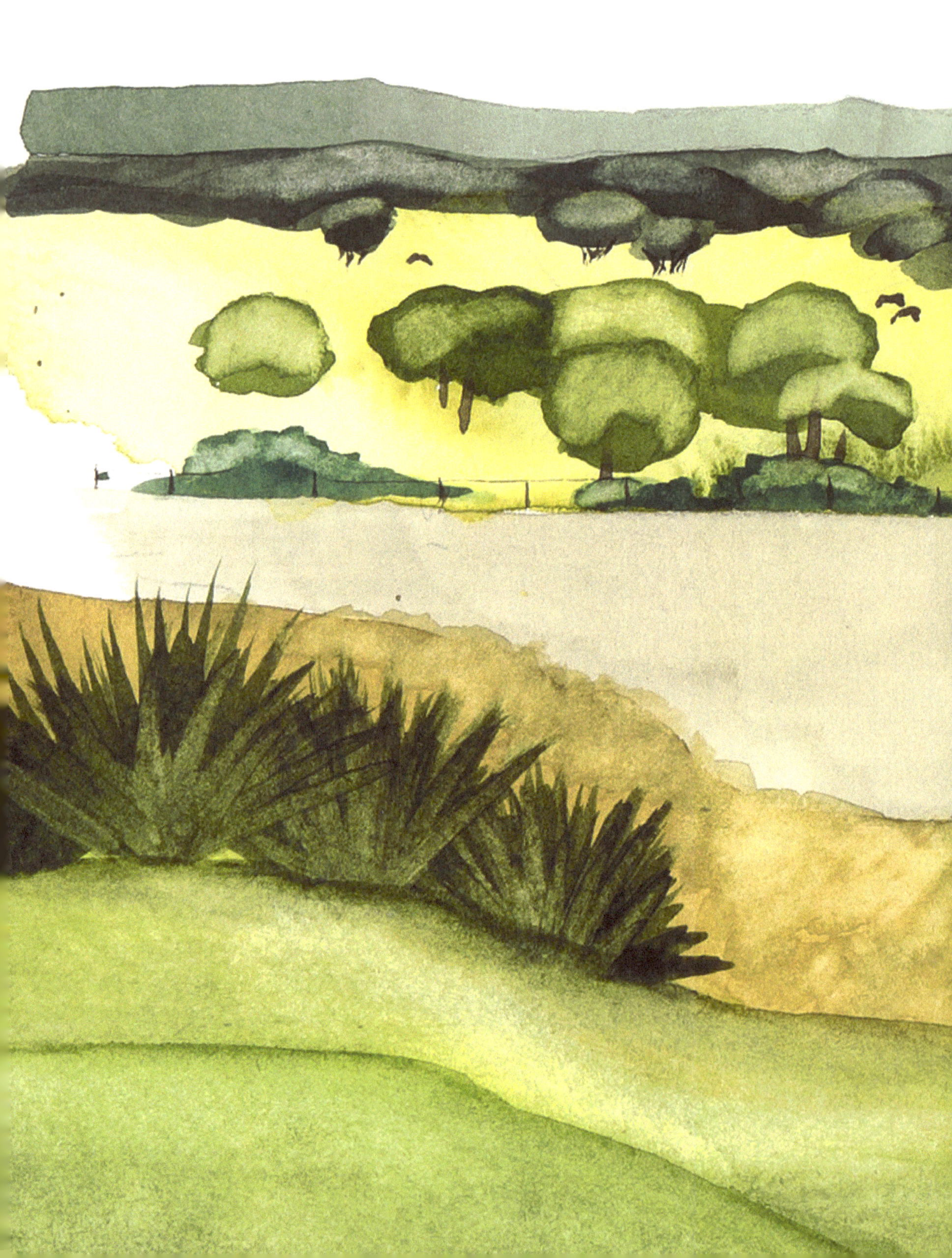

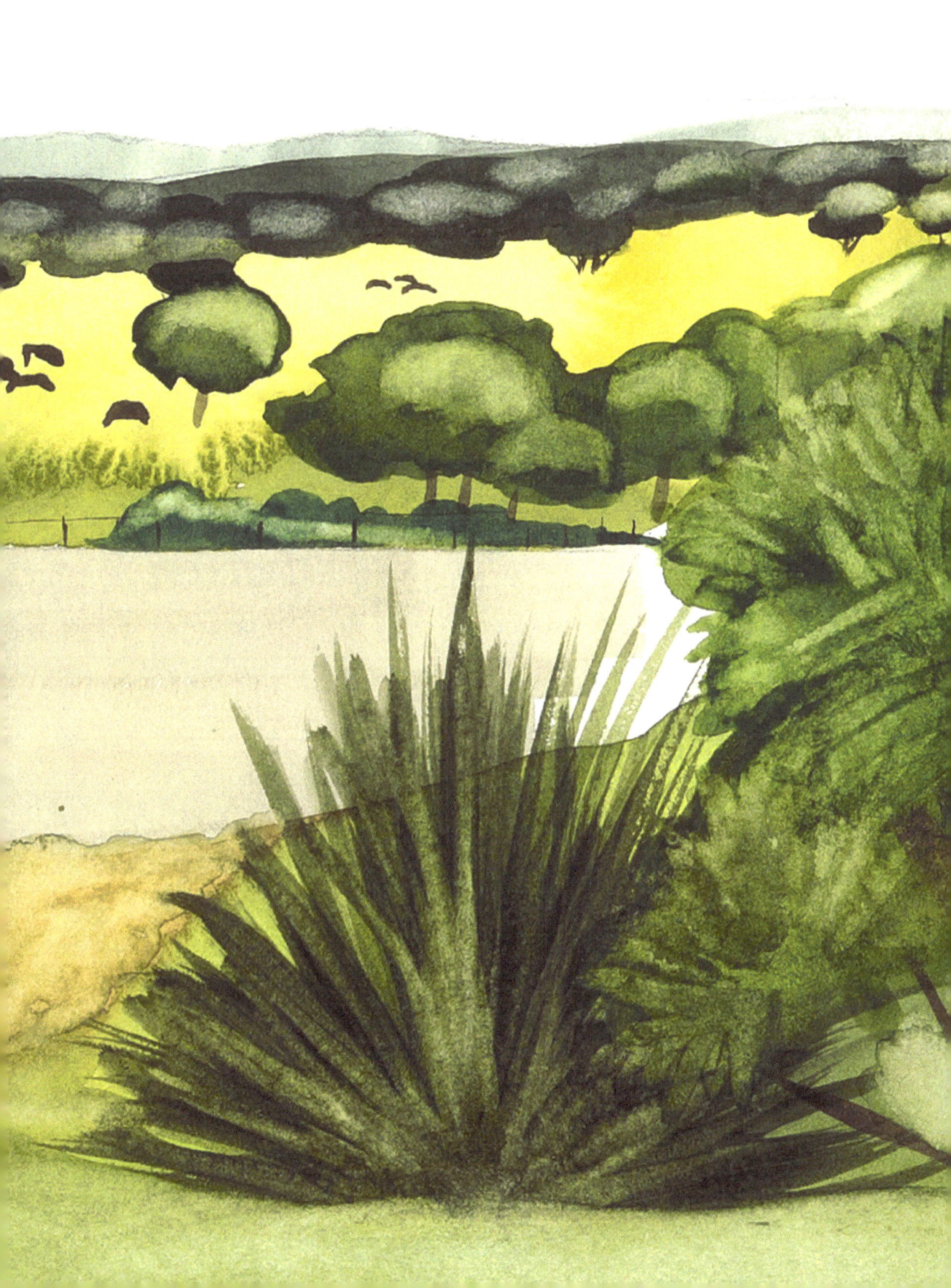

There are mysteries aplenty to be found here: the shimmering crescent moon in the dark clear sky, the cool August days, the beautiful hummingbirds, and the amazing mountains of Big Bend that rise up and create a universe unto itself in the high Texas desert. In Marfa, unidentified lights can be spotted in the distance as they come out on a clear night. They're small, and they bob up and down, turn red, and disappear—I've seen them myself. There is even an official light viewing station, outfitted in the tasteful style of the national parks, with exhibits and self-composting public restrooms. The lights have been studied and speculated upon, there are records of people seeing them from the 19th Century onwards, and most people around Marfa are content to leave them a mystery.

Actually, I don't live near West Texas, where Marfa and Big Bend are; I live near San Antonio. A friend of mine says Texas is Mexico without the turista and dysentery. I don't agree. I have traveled in Mexico, and Texas is different. It is to Mexico what Mexico is to Spain: that is, a hybrid with a character all its own. San Antonio has beautiful old missions and buildings and a river running through it that has been developed for the tourists who flock here. If you go north you hit the Hill Country, which was settled by German artisans and intellectuals about 150 years ago. The towns there—New Braunfels, Fredericksburg—contain the orchards, vineyards, and craft stores that reflect that influence.

The best thing about the Hill Country is the rivers, which flow through natural limestone deposits and clean themselves continuously. They're clear and cool and in some cases seasonal; they can go from raging torrents of water 30 feet wide to a trickle within a few months. Blue herons, raccoons, ducks, deer, turkey, scissortail, water snakes, turtles, ringtail cats, coyotes, and people enjoy their waters. We live on a little river north of San Antonio, on a hill overlooking the surrounding valley. Occasionally it reminds me of pictures I've seen of Africa. San Antonio is growing north and threatening to gobble us up, but for now our valley is safe. We float our river almost every day from April to August.

Sometimes we drive south to the Texas Gulf Coast, which is an acquired taste. I have always loved the salt-filled waters and water-filled breezes. Beaches on the barrier islands can go on for hundreds of miles, and you can even drive on them. People from all over enjoy this coast. The well-to-do have homes on man-made canals with giant fishing yachts parked in front of them. Other families stay in motels or camp right on the beach, wading out into the waters with fishing poles and casting lines into the waves. Birds abound, fish jump, the wind blows, and refineries are visible in the distance. In this world, people and nature coexist; it is not ideal, but it is vital. We sometimes go to Port Aransas, a small tourist town on Padre Island, and stay with friends. We ride in their boat up the shipping channel and swim and water ski—that is, our 89-year-old hostess water skis. That's another reason I like Texas: old women have a lot of spirit here. They wear makeup and low-cut shirts; they water ski and shoot guns. They don't give up. Sometimes they write books that very few people read. My great aunt was an artist who created paintings no one wanted and wrote long treatises on her life and family. She had no children, and I imagine only a handful of people have read her works, but I admire her for recording her experiences. Texas gives you permission to live with passion.

And then there's Mexico. Living in Texas, you have a lot of influence of Mexican culture, food, music, language and people. But the best thing of all is Mexico itself. It is two-and-a-half hours from where we live, and it is exotic and entirely different from our country. With a little effort you can figure out the rules of engagement and set out on your own odyssey. Mexico is like India, only more visceral and fun loving; like Spain, only more tolerant and funky; like the American Southwest, only more culturally intact; like Tuscany, only less predictable; like the Alps, only with bougainvillea; like Hawaii, only cheaper; and like the Caribbean, only friendlier. It is a great country, and it's right next to Texas.

I used to not like Dallas. That was when I just drove through on my way home to San Antonio from Iowa, where we lived for 18 years. But then the Dallas Museum of Art featured my daughter's art for 6 months in a show about upcoming Texas artists. I went to the opening, enjoyed a party at a prominent collector's house, and visited the Fort Worth Modern Art Museum, the new Nasher Sculpture Center, and the Dallas Symphony. Now I think of it as a destination city with many cultural events to enjoy.

San Antonio is currently booming. It is not the sleepy town of 500,000 people I grew up in. It is inhabited by well over a million people now, many from other parts of the United States and many of Hispanic descent. There are hundreds of Mexican restaurants, with the best food in the nation. There are rivers, missions, shopping malls, and giant venues for sports and conferences. There are beautiful historic neighborhoods and ever-new developments in the hills, which form the northern boundary of the city. Every spring the city engages in a 10-day-long super-party called "Fiesta," which is a little like Mardi Gras but more family-friendly. Fiesta features three parades: the River Parade (mainly barges with bands), the Fiesta Flambeau (a night parade), and the Battle of Flowers (a parade with military marching bands and "Duchesses" with the most elaborate dresses ever created—and I mean that seriously—you'll have to come and see for yourself). Countless street fairs, coronations of Kings and Queens, and private parties abound. There are Mariachi musicians everywhere, creating an atmosphere of happiness and closeness. There is a cultural value here that "Life is a Gift" to be enjoyed and shared with your loved ones. Young people respect their elders, and that is probably because their elders are still having fun. I've seen white-haired couples on the dance floor getting down to the music of a funky soul band from Fort Worth and old ladies getting on the bus to go to the Missions for an all-night party. One of my favorite images is of the families who camp out under the freeway (next to the bleachers that have been set up for attendees with tickets) to bring their families to watch the Battle of Flowers parade. They have tents, their own Porta Potties, outdoor grills, and makeshift seats. They camp for days and then bring 80 to 100 family members and friends to the area for an all-day party to see first the day parade and then the Saturday night Fiesta Flambeau. Every organization has its event, float, and "Fiesta medal." People go around town wearing sashes laden with the medals they've collected—like Girl Scout medals, only *these* are party medals! You gotta love it.

I think I'll stay in Texas. It's the place I want to be buried. My family has a plot in the cemetery on a hill in the south part of town overlooking the San Antonio River. There is a simple granite cross with my maiden name, Bain, carved into it. My grandparents are buried there (1932, 1938), as well as my father (1969), my brother (2000), and my mother (2003). I want my husband next to me. After being married as long as we have (40 years this summer), I feel that it's only fair—I don't want to look like a spinster. But he wants his ashes to go into Lake Tahoe, or maybe the Ganges River, where we visited this year (that was an experience, and another story). We're negotiating. Meanwhile, we're still enjoying this gift of life, hoping for grandchildren, going to Fiesta, and planning another road trip West this summer to attend our son's commencement from graduate school. We will visit the lake, play a couple of concerts, and pay our respects once again to the grand West we love so much.

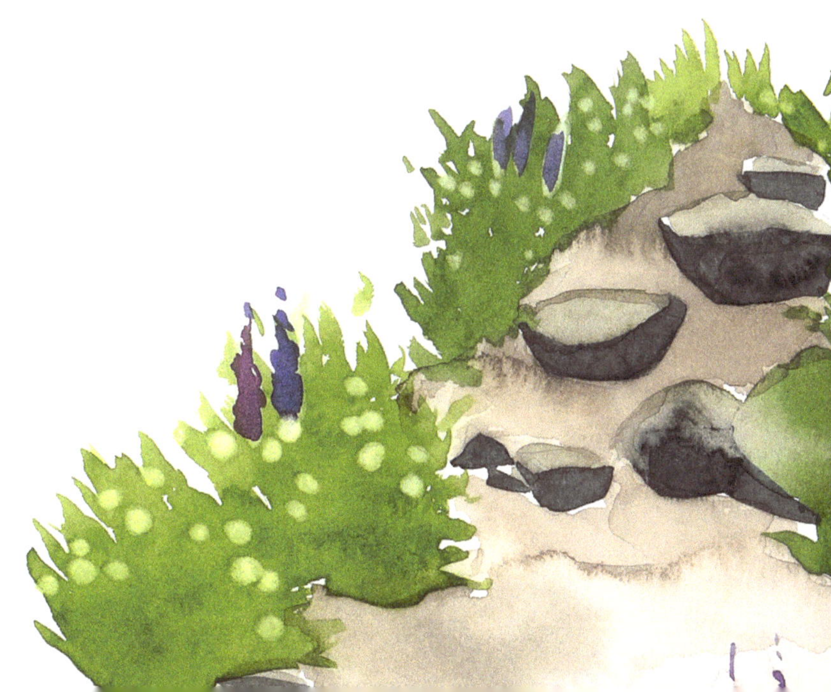

EPILOGUE *Fall 2012*

Nothing stays the same, that's a given. Still, some changes bear mentioning. The most important thing that has changed for me is that I have become the grandmother of two beautiful boys, Brendan and Paul, who are truly the lights of my life.

Another positive change involves *The Loading Zone*, Paul's band from the 60's profiled in *Reunion II*. There was a second version of the band that recorded one album independently and featured a fabulous jazz drummer named George Marsh that Paul never forgot. Paul reconnected with him and the bass player and they released an amazing CD, called *Blue Flame* (available on Amazon) which includes 5 new songs and 3 from the album recorded in 1969. Paul's singing and playing on those old songs was wild, energetic, assertive and sexy—in other words—young! The new music sounds wise and beautiful and a little wistful—in other words—ah, I don't want to say it!

Change for the worse is harder to look in the eye, but I feel compelled to mention something about the wonderful country of Mexico, which is only 2 and ½ hours from where we live. The Drug Cartels have made it unsafe to travel in certain parts of Mexico, particularly the northern states. The US State Department has even issued travel warnings although it is apparently possible to fly into the lavish resorts along the coastlines without problems. This has put a stop to our trips into the interior of Mexico for the time being. We are hoping things will resolve themselves in a positvie manner and Mexico will begin to flourish again.

Finally, Oprah has made meditation fashionable again and we have been called out of retirement to teach Transcendental Meditation in our home city of San Antonio. It is rewarding and reconnects us to people, places and organizations we spent so much time with in the past.

So my spiral theory—history repeating itself in slightly different ways—is proving relevant. I am nanny to my grandchildren, a TM teacher, and am preparing to travel across the globe to visit our son and his wife who have moved to Beijing, China. Stay tuned.

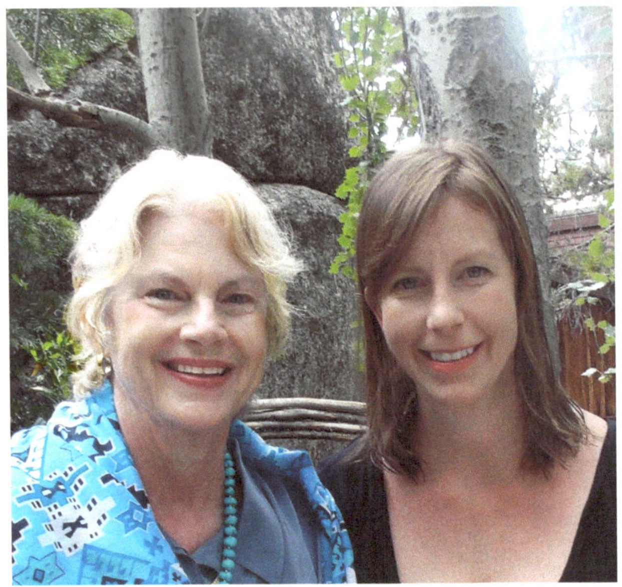

ABOUT

Josephine Bain Fauerso returned to her native San Antonio in 2000. She is a writer, traveler, educator, mother and grandmother who currently lives with her husband of 44 years in San Antonio. Her daughter, Joey Fauerso, created the watercolors for this book.

Joey Fauerso is an artist who has exhibited her paintings and animations nationally and internationally. She is an Assistant Professor of Art at Texas State University, and lives with her husband and two sons in San Antonio, Texas.

ACKNOWLEDGEMENTS

First and foremost, I would like to thank my daughter, Joey Fauerso for her amazing water colors that bring my essays so vividly to life. I would also like to thank Devi Norton for her beautiful book design, Scott Robinson for his careful editing, Marilyn Goldhaber for the picture above, and *The Iowa Source* for publishing several of the essays when they were written. And of course I must give a special thanks to my husband, Paul, for driving me through all of the amazing places in the American West and our children for going with us on most of our trips. Finally I would like to thank my father for starting this whole process with his intrepid leadership of family road trips with the rowdiest of participants.

www.ingramcontent.com/pod-product-compliance
Lightning Source LLC
LaVergne TN
LVHW070216110826
845147LV00003B/585
* 9 7 8 0 9 8 2 9 8 2 3 3 4 *